Debating the Constitution

Debating the Constitution

*New Perspectives on Constitutional
Reform*

Edited by

Anthony Barnett, Caroline Ellis and Paul Hirst

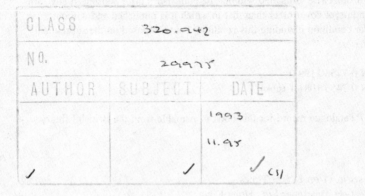
Polity Press

Copyright © this collection Polity Press 1993
Preface © Caroline Ellis
Each chapter copyright © the author.

First published in 1993 by Polity Press
in association with Blackwell Publishers

Editorial office:
Polity Press
65 Bridge Street
Cambridge CB2 1UR, UK

Marketing and production:
Blackwell Publishers
108 Cowley Road
Oxford OX4 1JF, UK

238 Main Street
Cambridge, MA 02142, USA

ISBN 0 7456 1199 0
ISBN 0 7456 1081 1 (pbk)

A CIP catalogue record for this book is available from the British Library.

Typeset in 11 on 12½ pt Times
by Best-set Typesetter Ltd., Hong Kong
Printed in Great Britain by T.J. Press (Padstow) Ltd., Padstow, Cornwall

This book is printed on acid-free paper.

Contents

The Contributors

Yasmin Ali is Senior Lecturer in Politics in the Department of Historical and Critical Studies, and Faculty Adviser on Equal Opportunities, University of Central Lancashire.

Anthony Barnett is Co-ordinator of Charter 88. A writer and journalist, he is the author of *Aftermath* with John Pilger (1981), *Iron Britannia* (1983) and *Soviet Freedom* (1988).

Tony Benn is Labour MP for Chesterfield. He was MP for Bristol South East 1950–83 and has been on the National Executive Committee of the Labour Party since 1959. He has contested the Labour leadership twice, in 1976 and 1988. He has been a cabinet minister in every Labour government since 1964. His diaries for 1963–90 have been published in five volumes.

David Byrne is a former community worker who now teaches in the Department of Sociology and Social Policy, University of Durham. He is a Labour councillor in Gateshead and is a member of the Campaign for a Northern Assembly.

Richard Corbett is Policy Adviser to the Socialist Group in the European Parliament on constitutional matters. He has written widely on European Affairs and is co-author of *The European Parliament* (2nd edition, 1992).

James Cornford is Director of the Institute for Public Policy Research. He is the Literary Editor of *Political Quarterly* and Chair of the Council of the Campaign for Freedom of Information. He was Professor of Politics at Edinburgh University 1968–76 and is a former Director of the Nuffield Foundation.

Nicholas Deakin is Professor of Social Policy and Administration at Birmingham University. He is a former civil servant and local government officer, and author of *The Enterprise Culture and the Inner Cities* (1993).

Caroline Ellis is a former writer with *New Statesman and Society*. She co-ordinated the workshops at the Manchester convention in 1991 and organized the Charter 88 Trust's conference on gender and power, 'Can Democracy Work for Women?', in November 1992. She is Charter 88's Political Officer.

Peter Hain is Labour MP for Neath. He was Labour parliamentary candidate for Putney in 1983 and 1987 and is Secretary of the Tribune Group of MPs. His books include *Proportional Misrepresentation* (1986).

Robert Hazell is a former senior civil servant with the Home Office. Whilst a barrister for the National Council of Civil Liberties he wrote *The Bar on Trial* (1974), which urged radical reform of the bar and its restrictive practices. He is currently Director of the Nuffield Foundation, which he joined in May 1989.

David Held is Professor of Politics and Sociology at the Open University, and the author of *Models of Democracy* (1987) and *Political Theory and the Modern State* (1989), among other recent works.

Paul Hirst was Director of Charter 88's 1991 constitutional convention and is a member of Charter 88's Executive. He is the author of *After Thatcher* (1989) and *Representative Democracy and its Limits* (1990) and is Professor of Social Theory at Birkbeck College, University of London.

Andrew Hood is a political researcher, journalist and teacher who is co-author, with Tony Benn MP, of two forthcoming books. The first, an analysis of the British constitution, will be published in June.

Sally Hughes is a barrister and journalist. She worked for the Legal Action Group 1981–6. She is the author of the Law Society report *The Circuit Bench – A Woman's Place?* (1991), and of numerous articles on the legal profession and the impact of the law on women and society. She contributes regularly to the national and specialist press.

Will Hutton is Economics Editor of *The Guardian* and a member of the Charter 88 Council.

Gus John is Director of Education in the London Borough of Hackney and a former Head of Community Education for the Inner London Education Authority. He has conducted several studies into race and the inner city and was co-author of the Burnage Report, *Murder in the Playground* (1989). He is a founder member of European Action for Racial Equality and Social Justice.

Francesca Klug is currently a Research Fellow of the Human Rights Centre at Essex University where she is working on *The Democratic Audit of the UK*. She was formerly Director of the Civil Liberties Trust, the charitable research arm of Liberty. She has written on race, immigration and gender, and was the prime author of 'A People's Charter', Liberty's bill of rights, published in October 1991.

Anthony Lester QC is a leading human rights advocate practising at the English Bar. He has argued many of the leading British cases before the European Commission and Court of Human Rights as well as in Britain. He was Special Adviser to the Home Secretary, Roy Jenkins, between 1974 and 1976 with responsibility for developing policy on sex and race discrimination legislation and constitutional reform. He is President of Interights and Chairman of the Runnymede Trust, and was Chairman of the Institute for Public Policy Research working party on a bill of rights (1991).

Isobel Lindsay is Convenor of the Campaign for a Scottish Assembly and a member of the Executive of the Scottish Constitutional Convention. She is a Lecturer in the Department of Government at Strathclyde University.

Ruth Lister is Professor of Applied Social Studies at the University of Bradford. She is a former Director of the Child Poverty Action Group. She is the author of *The Female Citizen* (1989), *The Exclusive Society: Citizenship and the Poor* (1990) and *Women's Economic Dependency and Social Security* (1992).

John Macdonald QC is a human rights lawyer and Chair of the Liberal Democrat Lawyers. He supported the Banabans people in the Ocean Island case; Yuri Orlov, the Chair of the Moscow Helsinki Monitoring Group; and the Canadian Indians who tried to stop Prime Minister Trudeau repatriating the Canadian Constitution.

David Marquand is Professor of Politics at Sheffield University and a former Labour MP. He is the author of *The Unprincipled Society* (1988) and *The Progressive Dilemma* (1991).

Michael Meadowcroft is Chair of the Electoral Reform Society. He was Liberal MP for Leeds West 1983–7 and Senior Visiting Fellow at the Policy Studies Institute in 1989.

Elizabeth Meehan is Professor of Politics and Jean Monnet Professor of European Social Policy at Queen's University, Belfast, and a Trustee of the Charter 88 Trust. She is the author of *Women's Rights at Work* (1985) and a forthcoming book on citizenship and the European Community.

Austin Mitchell is Labour MP for Great Grimsby. He is a former front-bench spokesman on Trade and Industry (1987–9), fired for presenting *Target*, a political discussion programme on Sky. He was a Fellow of Nuffield College, then a television journalist. His books include *Westminster Man* (1984), *Britain Beyond the Blue Horizon* (1989), *Competitive Socialism* (1989) and *Full Employment in a Free Society* (1991).

Geoff Mulgan is Director of DEMOS. He was previously Policy Adviser to Gordon Brown MP, the Shadow Chancellor. He is the author of *Saturday Night or Sunday Morning* (1987) with Ken Worpole, and *Communication and Control* (1991).

Jean Seaton is the author of *Power without Responsibility* (1991) with James Curran, and editor of *The Media in British Politics* with Ben Pimlott. She teaches at South Bank University.

Sarah Spencer is a Research Fellow at the Institute for Public Policy Research and a former General Secretary of the National Council for Civil Liberties. She has written widely on civil liberty issues, and is a co-author of IPPR's publications *A British Bill of Rights* (1990) and *The Constitution of the United Kingdom* (1991).

Frank Vibert is the Director and co-founder of the European Policy Forum (set up in April 1992) for British and European Market Studies. He was previously Deputy Director of the Institute of Economic Affairs and edited *Britain's Constitutional Future* (1991).

Marina Warner is a critic, novelist and broadcaster. Her books include *Monuments and Maidens* (1985) and *Indigo* (1992). She is a member of Charter 88's Executive, and sits on the Management Committee of the National Council for One-Parent Families and the Literature Panel of the Arts Council.

Preface

Caroline Ellis

Few debates in British politics in recent years have made such an impact as that over the constitution. This volume is both a comprehensive guide to the ideas and arguments which fuel this debate and an exploration of the ways in which constitutional reform would alter public (and in many instances private) life in the United Kingdom. Its contributions are drawn from the constitutional convention held in Manchester in November 1991 by Charter 88 and *The Independent*.

The current constitutional position of Britain is now challenged on two sides. On the one hand, it is subject to considerable external pressures from European integration (as documented by Richard Corbett in chapter 22 on the European constitution) and wider global economic and political trends towards interdependence (described in chapter 23 by David Held). On the other hand, pressure for change is building up from below. Increasing numbers of people now believe not only that the foundations of British democracy are shaky and inadequate but that our system of governance itself is rotten to the core. Their anger at our misrule is channelled into a positive agenda for change.

While both these factors increase the likelihood of a new constitutional settlement, they also present challenges for reformers. If Europe is undermining traditional British views on the distribution of power in our constitution, there is still the thorny problem of how power can be shared effectively between different tiers of government and at what level specific political and economic decisions are best taken. Moreover, the fact that there is popular momentum behind demands for change does not guarantee the creation of a political consensus around a particular reform package.

These and other challenges raised by the constitutional debate are confronted directly. The former is tackled in chapters on the police, the economy and the public services. Isobel Lindsay, in chapter 24, deals with the problem of gaining cross-party consensus for constitutional change in her discussion of moves towards devolution in Scotland, where opposition to the UK constitution has been strongest.

The Case for Constitutional Reform

What is the case against our current constitutional arrangements? The argument made repeatedly in this book is that a modern democracy cannot function as it should if power is concentrated in one place. Contributions from people of many different backgrounds and political traditions pinpoint the doctrine of the absolute sovereignty of Parliament, which lies at the heart of the Westminster system of government, as the source of many of Britain's current woes. Upon closer inspection, parliamentary sovereignty turns out be a thin veil for a more insidious form of largely unaccountable power wielded by the executive. The spirit which animates the reformers is a desire for shared power and citizenship rights, not only to halt abuses of our civil liberties but in order to make government answerable for all its actions and to encourage wider participation in government and public life. The premise of a written constitution would be popular rather than parliamentary or executive sovereignty. In other words, the subjects of Her Majesty's government would become citizens and all power and authority would derive from them. (The fate of Her Majesty herself in the event of the establishment of a written constitution is a moot point.)

As Anthony Lester QC indicates in chapter five on a bill of rights, the shift from subject to citizen involves the establishment of a framework of civil, political and human rights and their entrenchment against the wills or whims of bureaucrats and politicians. In addition, as three campaigners for (three different kinds of) electoral reform show in Part III, it means a voting system based on the principle of one person, one vote, *one value*. Under our current electoral system the value of the vote one casts depends on which part of the country one lives in. In the 1992 general election, for example, Labour polled a total of 1.5 million votes in 16 out of the 38 shire counties, yet none of the 115 MPs elected in those areas was Labour. However, in 11 major cities Labour polled a total of 1.44 million votes and obtained 54 out of 65 MPs. Under a proportional electoral system far fewer votes would be wasted and each vote cast would count more equally. Government would be more truly representative as a result.

Further, most contributors are agreed that state power should be shared between different institutions and different levels of government (whether national in the case of Scotland, Wales and Northern Ireland, regional or local), on the basis that decisions should be taken at the lowest practicable level (the subsidiarity principle). This principle applies equally well to those decisions which we need to pool with other members of the European Community.

More than any specific grievance there is the feeling that, without democratic renewal, not only will civil liberties be further eroded but so will any sense of social solidarity and economic confidence. The debate over the constitution is not simply about how we govern ourselves; it is about the kind of society we want to become. For, as Elizabeth Meehan points out in chapter 8 on women's rights in citizens' Europe, a written constitution would encourage a culture of rights and citizenship that would inspire and empower people in all kinds of ways in their everyday lives.

What Kind of Constitution?

In Part I of this collection we sample the different reform programmes on offer. Two of these proposals have been presented as draft constitutions – the Institute for Public Policy Research's (IPPR) 'The Constitution of the United Kingdom' and the Liberal Democrats' 'We the People ... Towards a Written Constitution'; another has been presented as a parliamentary bill Tony Benn's Commonwealth of Britain Bill – and a fourth as a discussion paper by Frank Vibert, Director of the European Policy Forum (formerly Deputy Director of the Institute of Economic Affairs). Here the respective authors describe their distinctive contribution to the reform debate.

James Cornford for the IPPR adopts in chapter one a comprehensive approach to the constitution. His draft revolutionizes the relationship between local, regional and national government, puts forward detailed proposals for judicial reform and the appointments of public officials, and broadens the scope of traditional bills of rights. John Macdonald QC in chapter two readily admits the shortcomings of the

Liberal Democrat draft by comparison (which draws exclusively on the European Convention for its bill of rights and does not entrench the right to know), but sees a virtue in specifying how reform can be brought about. 'We the People' proposes a schedule for reform lasting six years.

Tony Benn in chapter three has a rather different project in mind. He perceives the struggle over the constitution as one between the powerful and the dispossessed. For this reason he does not follow the classic liberal democratic model of a separation of powers. His bill would bring an end to absolute executive power and restore genuine parliamentary sovereignty. The power of the courts to provide redress for abuses of power by democratically elected politicians would be greatly reduced, since Benn considers the ballot box to be the main guarantor of our freedoms.

At the opposite end of the political spectrum, Frank Vibert (an advocate of the free market) in chapter four adopts a softly-softly attitude to proportional representation and rights but a robust approach to the business of government itself, arguing for a reappraisal of what motivates ministers and civil servants. Vibert prefers incremental, evolutionary change to sudden reform.

Indeed, most agree that to some extent we have to work on what is already there – we cannot start again from the beginning. As Marina Warner writes in chapter 26, Charter 88 grows out of traditions of civil liberty and tolerance while seeking to change them. Existing institutions and conventions would be transformed rather than abolished. The House of Commons would be elected on a different basis; local government's former limited autonomy would be not only restored but augmented and entrenched in a charter of autonomy. The United Kingdom once had metropolitan authorities; instead of reviving this model we would move towards regional governments for England as a whole, with regions gaining new powers not exercised by local authorities and taking over some powers from county councils. And what of British traditions of liberty and tolerance? Why not apply them to our own system of government (to quote the opening line of the declaration signed at the Manchester convention)? Francesca Klug, in her presentation in chapter six of the case for democratic entrenchment of a bill of rights, refers to the need to revive this concern for fairness and liberty in order to inspire people to defend actively the rights they have on paper.

In some cases it is a question of looking to traditions which metropolitanism has suppressed. For example, Isobel Lindsay argues that England could do worse than to learn from Scotland, which has a longer tradition of democratic rights and a more robust sense of collective values. Here it has been possible to build a powerful and broad-based coalition of social and political groupings around the campaign for a Scottish parliament, a bill of rights and equal representation for women. In similar vein, David Byrne documents in chapter 21 the growing desire of the north east to assert its own identity, resist the imperatives of the City of London and the south east, and take control of its own economic future. And in her discussion in chapter 20 of the relationship between the media and the constitution, Jean Seaton expresses the hope that we will not allow all that is good about our unique system of public service broadcasting to be swept away by the undiscerning market forces which increasingly seek to dominate our cultural life.

Disestablishing the Establishment

In Part V, Nicholas Deakin (chapter 17) emphasizes that if the United Kingdom is to become a modern European democracy, the establishment will have to be disestablished and many kinds of institution in society will have to change in style, composition and culture. In this context, he argues, we need a fundamental reappraisal of the way we run our public services: how much decentralization should there be? What should be the balance between democracy and efficiency? How should we reward innovation? Robert Hazell in chapter 16 is more pragmatic. He advises against waiting for wholesale constitutional change before tackling Civil Service reform, proposing four simple measures which could be taken without any new legislation. But he too is motivated by the desire to improve our rights as citizens, not just as customers. Turning to the place of the police in our constitution, Sarah Spencer in chapter 19 describes the detail of the IPPR's proposals, which centre on the need to reassert democratic control and accountability, particularly at local level. In her discussion of the judiciary in chapter 18, Sally Hughes urges a more searching approach to the issue of judicial reform. Reformers must end their obsession with the pronouncements of judges at the top of the tree and instead look at what is going on at the grass roots – for it is here that the case for reform is most apparent and that ideas for change suggest themselves most readily.

Civil Society and Pluralism

At a time when racism, fascist groupings and ethnic conflict are on the rise in most European countries and when yet another backlash has begun against the successes of modern feminism and its supposed 'illiberalism', a number of contributors feel compelled to grapple with the issues of how definitions of citizenship can be broadened to include those previously on the outside, and of how we ensure equal rights, irrespective of our different identities. Any new constitutional settlement would be based on pluralism; but exactly what does this mean? Does it mean condoning unequal power relations and tolerating repression on ethnic and racial grounds? What will citizenship come to signify in the twenty-first century? Marina Warner writes that diaspora is the modern condition, and calls on us to use difference creatively. In her denunciation of patronage of black communities by the undemocratic state and of patriarchal relations within those communities, Yasmin Ali contends in chapter nine that a written constitution must seek to combat racism without entrenching a static definition of 'race' or 'ethnic group identity' that ignores tensions between men and women, young and old. Gus John in chapter 25 insists that the education system must address the experiences of disaffected black youth, and sees a role for constitutional rights in facilitating this. Elizabeth Meehan states her belief that a written constitution would empower women to challenge definitions of work and citizenship which privilege men. She favours a strategy that recognizes both those areas in which equal treatment is appropriate and effective and also those where positive action, or gender-specific measures, are necessary to achieve parity between the sexes.

Who Decides Our Rights?

Some of the most heated debates over the constitution have centred on the question of a bill of rights. Civil libertarians, such as Clare Short MP or Conor Gearty, have expressed grave concerns about transferring political power from elected representatives to a reactionary judiciary (which, they argue, would be the consequence of incorporating the European Convention on Human Rights into British law or of entrenching a bill of rights). There are two responses to this argument.

One comes from Anthony Lester QC, who argues that our liberties are being eroded because of the vast discretionary powers held by ministers and civil servants. Parliament has failed to give the judges the necessary tools to protect human rights; it must make amends by passing a bill of rights, which would guide and educate judges in these matters. The judiciary can and should be reformed, but it has shown itself capable of the task at hand. The second response comes from Francesca Klug, who suggests that a bill of rights need not involve making judges the final arbiter when different rights come into conflict. Drawing on the Canadian model, she offers a method of entrenchment which both preserves the involvement of elected representatives in deciding the law on civil and political rights and ensures that we can use the courts to gain effective redress for infringements of human rights.

The Relationship Between Political and Economic Power

A further impetus to the cause of constitutional change is the growing crisis of our economic system, a crisis which existing political institutions are incapable of resolving. Will Hutton in chapter 13 likens the position of the central government to that of rentier landlords who can do as they like with the resources at their disposal: the absence of accountable and open structures encourages short-termism and manipulation of economic policy for narrow political ends. David Marquand in chapter 14 sees the hierarchical nature of our constitution as a barrier to the more collaborative form of capitalism represented by Germany and Scandinavia. The pluralization of state power would enable the kinds of cooperative economic network to develop which have made it possible for these economies to prosper. By way of contrast, Frank Vibert argues that constitutional change would reinforce the free market principle.

Geoff Mulgan in chapter 15 and Ruth Lister in chapter seven look at the ways in which the economy and the welfare system respectively might themselves be democratized. Both launch an attack on the public/private divide. A written constitution which left the market entirely to its own devices would not be worth the paper it was on. Mulgan argues that the greatest asset the modern company can have is its human capital, which it should invest in by empowering workers to take more control over decision making and to gain new skills. Lister argues that a firm bedrock of social and economic rights is essential if political and civil rights are to be exercised effectively. This requires action on three parallel levels: the incorporation of broad principles of social rights at constitutional level, backed up by a more detailed charter and implemented by means of detailed legislation.

Conclusion

It will now be clear that in spite of the growing convergence of opinion on the need for a radical overhaul of the UK constitution, there are still varying expectations of what constitutional reform might bring. The achievement of Charter 88 has been to channel these tensions creatively. Charter 88 seeks not only to deepen citizenship but to extend and rework this concept to make it relevant to all sections of society. Above all it seeks to draw attention to the relationship between the constitution and other areas of social life; for if there is a unifying factor in the debate over the constitution, it is the view that constitutional reform is an essential prerequisite for progressive politics and social emancipation. Once the central plank of our unwritten constitution has been removed, namely the concentration of all power in the executive, power can be dispersed and new spaces for popular participation can be opened up. Then, and only then, can we begin to think seriously about transforming the landscape of Britain from one of epochal decline to one of growth, invention and creativity.

Acknowledgements

We would like to thank The Joseph Rowntree Reform Trust and *The Independent* and its editor, Andreas Whittam Smith, for their invaluable support of the Manchester Convention, and the Joseph Rowntree Charitable Trust for its help on the editing costs of this book. The Proceedings of the Convention, with 110 pages of reports on all its sessions and a full list of all those whose work made it possible, is available price £8.95 from Charter 88 Trust Publications, Exmouth House, 3-11 Pine Street, London EC1R 0JH.

has confirmed the need for constitutional change. These events varied
in their nature, from the European Parliament elections in 1989 when
the Greens obtained 15 per cent of the vote and failed to get one of the
81 seats, to the Guildford Four and Birmingham Six scandals that
stained the record of British justice.

Charter 88 has made constitutional reform more than a narrow technical matter and a concern of insiders. Constitutional reform is sym-
bolic of social and political renewal, but outside of ideologies and
narrow party political positions. It answers diverse needs: that national
and local aspirations be recognized and provided with appropriate
political institutions free of the constraints of Westminster centralism,
that our electoral system be fair and not discriminate against millions of
voters, that our system of justice be above reproach, and that the laws
protect the rights of the citizen against encroachment by the state.

The convention was designed to reflect that broad perception of the
agenda and role of constitutional reform. Thus it contained a strong
cultural element, including a remarkable plenary at which Alan
Bleasdale, Isobel Lindsay, Ben Okri and Marina Warner all gave
speeches that ranged from the powerful to the electrifying on what
Britain would be like with a democratic culture. The convention also
explicitly sought to bring the political parties together, encouraging
rational debate of common issues between Labour, Conservative and
Liberal Democrat reformers, rather than competitive sloganizing. Thus
the opening plenary, chaired by Beverly Anderson, included Patricia
Hewitt, Will Hutton, Ferdinand Mount and Des Wilson. The central
plenary of the convention brought together the four major proposers of
draft constitutions for Britain – Tony Benn MP, James Cornford of the
IPPR (Institute for Public Policy Research), John Macdonald, the principal architect of the Liberal Democrat's draft constitution, and Frank
Vibert, then of the Institute of Economic Affairs. This session, chaired
by Geoffrey Robertson QC, showed that it is possible strongly to debate
the issues from different positions whilst finding common ground.
Indeed, it is obvious that no constitution can hope to last that cannot
command widespread assent, and for that to happen left, right and
centre will have to be able to talk with one another and not merely
disagree. Manchester showed that they can, despite the official parties.
In this sense it was no mere conference, but had the feel of a true
constitutional convention, if not one with plenary drafting powers.

The convention was valuably supported by *The Independent* and was
the culmination of the first phase of Charter 88's activities. It put both

the organization and the issue indelibly on the political map, and it scotched the sneers of hostile elements in the media and the parties that it was the exclusive concern of Hampstead intellectuals and had no resonance with non-metropolitan, non-elite citizens. The convention was conceived in the Charter's first plan. This was outlined in our January 1990 strategy document 'Prospects and Plans for the Nineties' and was preceded by a very successful one-day event in London on 14 July 1990, 'Make a Date with Democracy'.

It was followed by an event that had not been long planned, but which stemmed from the convention's capacity to pull in large numbers of concerned citizens – Democracy Day. On 2 April 1992, Charter 88 groups hosted over a hundred meetings in constituencies across the country at which parliamentary candidates from all the parties debated the issue of constitutional reform. Many of those meetings were packed, several attracting audiences in the hundreds. The meetings were the largest and liveliest *real* event during a lacklustre general election campaign. Several candidates from the major parties remarked that only Charter 88 had the capacity to pull in genuine audiences of interested voters, people who had got on the bus to go there because they cared about the issues rather than being bussed in as party faithful to fill up artificial events and rallies. Constitutional reform became a major issue in the election campaign. This is probably the first time it has figured in this broad way, rather than in the form of Irish Home Rule or a Scottish assembly, since women's suffrage.

The Conservatives won the election, and many, therefore, see the issue of reforming the constitution as marginalized and inherently unlikely to retain its new relevance. Many argue that the demise of Margaret Thatcher as prime minister and John Major's premiership mean the end of intransigent, arbitrary and ruthlessly interventionist government, and with it an end to real concern about our political institutions. Decent chaps will go back to playing the game by the rules, honouring the unwritten constitutional conventions, and Major will set about restructuring cabinet government rather than personal rule. The 1992 election, it is widely argued, was reasonably fair. The Tories with 43 per cent of the vote have only a modest majority, not the crushing 100+ position they had on a similar percentage of the vote in 1983 and 1987. Labour on 35 per cent cannot reasonably challenge the legitimacy of the result.

Some people in the Labour Party have sought to blame the prominence given to constitutional issues in the campaign for their failure to win the election. They ignore the point that Labour *had* to respond to the growing saliency of these issues and, in particular, given the opinion polls almost universally pointing to the prospect of a hung Parliament, *had* to consider the issue of PR (proportional representation). Labour had moved an immense distance since the mid-1980s, gradually responding to constitutional issues like PR with the Plant Commission, and playing a major part in shaping others, like the Scottish Constitutional Convention's campaign for a Scottish assembly. The critics should ask themselves where Labour would have been had it ducked out of the constitutional agenda, remained rigidly unionist on Scotland, and offered voters wavering between them and the Liberal Democrats no prospect of change by utterly spurning PR. The outcome could hardly have been enhanced support.

Constitutional change certainly cannot come if Labour opposes it. But if Labour does so, it can hardly sustain its position as the main radical and reforming party. It will be relinquishing a claim on the future in favour of the habits of the past. Constitutional conservatives of all political colours feel relieved by the April 1992 result. They think the moment of danger has passed and that the age-old myths of the stability, continuity and particularity of British institutions can be wheeled out once more. But it will not do any more to play Mr Podsnap in the face of demands for reform in the United Kingdom.

The Conservatives' fourth election triumph has faded with an unprecedented rapidity. Floating voters decided the election and many seem to have made up their minds late in the campaign and, finally, to have chosen the 'safe' option, voting for cautious and economically competent government. So far they have got neither caution nor competence. The Conservatives this time inherited the crisis of their own making, and with it the hard choices they had avoided in the run-up to the election. Major has sought to compensate for the unpopularity of Thatcher by stressing collegiality in cabinet decision making and a more emollient style of government. However, he and his ministers have misread the mood of the people since August 1992, provoking a storm of protest over pit closures. They have shown a disastrous combination of initial dogmatism over policy and then vacillating weakness after its failure in the management of the economy. Major's government is isolated from the mood of Britain, as only a government walled up in Whitehall and attentive solely to its majority in Westminster can be when it goes off the tracks.

Constitutional issues are unlikely to be driven off the agenda by the mess the government has made; failure highlights the defects of our system of government. The farcical handling of the process of ratification of the Maastricht Treaty shows, for example, British institutions at their worst. The government refused a referendum, despite real divisions in opinion in both major parties and widespread concern in the country. The Danish and French referendums were the spur to debate in Britain, and most people here have never seen even an outline of the proposals in the Treaty. The government could only survive the initial vote in Parliament with Liberal Democrat support and by browbeating its own MPs – and then only by a majority of three.

A government on the ropes is one thing, but a fundamental crisis of the British state and its relation to society is another. Britain needs constitutional reform, but it faces neither the crisis of national political institutions, nor the galloping political corruption of Italy. We should be grateful that the whole of the United Kingdom is not racked by political violence, that government is carried on with a fair degree of competence by honest civil servants, that the political parties are not irrevocably divided by ideology and personality. Were that so, then the prospects for constitutional reform would be grim indeed. Peaceful constitutional reform is only a credible political project *because* there is some coherence to the British state and political system.

Britain does not have to have a political system on the point of collapse for constitutional issues to matter. The reverse is true. These issues matter when it is still possible for the parties to agree about them. They become irrelevant when there is little but total enmity. Britain needed constitutional change in the early 1980s as much as it does in the early 1990s. It was hardly spoken about, for the reason that a Labour Party on the verge of falling to the hard left had nothing but insults to throw at a Conservative Party dominated by Thatcher and the hard right.

Britain does have major political and social problems to which constitutional reform is the answer, not in the sense of a quick-fix solution but as the beginning of the process whereby they are tackled. The principal problem in Britain's institutions is the strong tendency to exclusive party government and its control of a highly centralized state with few checks on the executive. Exclusive government, concentrated in the hands of the prime minister and the Cabinet, narrowly confined in Whitehall and Westminster, has prevented the development of a collaborative political culture that makes possible the cooperation of the major social interests one with another and with the state. Policy has shifted substantially as new tenants have moved into 10 Downing Street; each administration undoing or further modifying the reforms of the one preceding. In recent years policy has shifted with equal frequency as new factions have risen to the top in the Conservative government. The result has been a fundamental failure of continuity in policy and institutions. The National Health Service, education and local government have suffered decades of meddling and restless 'reform'. The effects on morale and competence in local government have been near terminal, and education and health seem set to follow. Economic policy has suffered both from rapid changes of direction between administrations and from government's manipulation of the economy to fit in with the electoral cycle.

Constitutional reform as advocated by Charter 88 would decentralize government. It would also allow for a more collaborative political culture, as PR undermined the prize of exclusive party government. Both changes would lead to both greater consistency in policy and greater attention to a wider range of interests in forming it. More consistent and less partial government could not but create a climate of stability more favourable to economic performance than the zigzagging of policy in recent decades.

Britain is at the bottom of the G7 major advanced industrial countries on indicator after indicator, and close to the bottom of the Organization for Economic Cooperation and Development league table of 23 countries too. This is not a coincidence and cannot be blamed solely on British managers and unions. The United Kingdom needs fundamental reforms in its central governmental institutions in order to ensure accountability, stability and efficiency in policy. Radical reforms *at* the centre are needed in large measure to halt the process of half-baked and oft-reversed reform *from* the centre. Proportional representation, devolution and decentralization, and a written constitution would all assist in this matter.

The idea that what Britain truly needs is one more dose of really strong central government is absurd. Remember that the phrase 'elective dictatorship' to describe the British political system was revived by Lord Hailsham in the later 1970s when he feared a partisan *Labour* government. Elective dictatorship can as well be pursued by a government that carefully avoids the strident tones of Margaret Thatcher – indeed, better so. Thatcher exceeded the limits of what Britons were prepared to suffer from government when she drove through the poll tax in a classic demonstration of the defects of our institutions. She believed that Parliament is 'sovereign' and can pass any law not contrary to nature. She also believed that the prime minister has Parliament available as an always obedient tool, with a majority of supine MPs of her party willing to do whatever the whips bid them. These were fatal conceits, encouraged by the absurdities that pass for constitutional thought in Britain. But Britain for all its faults is a democracy and the people are not cowed by our defective institutions. Riots in unlikely places like Weston-super-Mare, widespread evasion, and fear of eventual electoral extermination killed the poll tax and ended Thatcher's premiership. John Major's government is a weak government, but we should be worried about a strong and flexible government exploiting the powers of the Westminster system to party advantage. A government that is intelligent enough not to believe the textbooks too much but to exploit the real unaccountable powers with due caution, that is not so stupid as to antagonize the majority of the nation on an issue close to their pockets, can expect to be obeyed. The poll tax came close to making a mockery of the rule of law, but it revealed how few restraints there are on the law-making powers of Parliament and on the authority and executive powers of government other than common prudence and the need to be re-elected. Elective dictatorship still exists, and it will not be curbed without major institutional changes – chief among which are PR and a bill of rights.

The other most important problem is that the rights of citizens are poorly protected by law in the United Kingdom and that there are few domestic remedies for a wide range of abuses of authority that are covered by statute law or the prerogative powers of the crown. An outline of the areas of concern would go on for pages; we can but list a few of the most outrageous instances of abuse. Trade union rights are denied to employees at GCHQ (Government Communications Headquarters) by ministerial fiat, the telephone conversations of law-abiding citizens like Harriet Harman or organizations of unquestionable integrity like Amnesty are intercepted. The sealing off of whole counties during the 1984–5 miners' strike and the creation of an exclusion zone around Stonehenge at the summer solstice show the police acting with indifference to internationally recognized rights of freedom of assembly and movement, and exploiting the provisions of draconian public order acts that are inappropriate to a peacetime democracy. Finally, there is the scandal of the all-too-many serious miscarriages of justice that have come to light, including the horrific cases of the Birmingham Six, Guildford Four and Tottenham Three. These cases stem from common causes: a politically inspired culture of neglect for and indifference to the rights of citizens that, mixed with ethnic prejudice, has enabled the police to abuse suspects and to extract false confessions by oppressive means.

This culture and these attitudes are beginning to end. A determined attempt is being made to deal with the backlog of serious miscarriages of justice and to address the problems of criminal procedure. W.G. Runciman's Royal Commission on Criminal Procedure is the first for many years. The inspector of prisons, Judge Stephen Tumin, has been tolerated in office, despite excoriating reports on the service. Lord Chief Justice Taylor clearly now seems to want to show that the judiciary is willing to check abuses. John Major's concept of citizen's charters shows the government is trying to treat the members of the public in a way that concedes that they can expect a certain standard of service, and reliefs should they fail to get it. All these cautious moves away from the state of seige mentality that prevailed in the early eighties are to be welcomed, but they can be no more than palliatives of a fundamentally deficient system of protection of citizens' rights. These abuses and scandals will only end when we have an entrenched bill of rights in theUnited Kingdom, which both limits the scope of legislation in matters of fundamental rights and offers the citizen reliefs at law in the case of the infringement of rights by the executive or its agents.

A bill of rights is a central part of the building of a culture of liberty among the citizens of the United Kingdom. Opinion poll data shows the mass of the population support a bill of rights. The problem is not our indifference to liberty as such but the relative poverty of many people's expectations about participation in democratic government and for their security from undue interference by government. The next task of the Charter 88 movement, and a vital part of its campaign for institutional change, is to transform this passivity and this poverty of expectation. More will be needed than a weekend convention or a day of meetings across the country. A long campaign of education and inquiry, conducted not by QCs or constitutional experts alone but by active citizens in Charter groups across the country, is what we need. This process has begun with the announcement of the Citizen's Enquiry. It will go on until early 1995. By then, Charter 88 will have ceased to be a campaigning organization, and will be a nationwide citizens' movement, committed to forcing constitutional change from the parties.

Part I

Towards a Written Constitution

1 The Case for Wholesale Constitutional Reform

James Cornford

Over the last twenty years there has been a growing chorus of complaint about aspects of British government which in any other system would be recognized as constitutional: that is, complaints of an electoral system which seriously distorts representation, and threatens to perpetuate rule by the largest minority party; of a Parliament which is dominated by the executive through its control of procedure and the disciplines of party, patronage and the press, and which therefore fails to scrutinize effectively the conduct of government or to play any constructive role in legislation; of a national administration which practices excessive secrecy and against whose actions there is inadequate redress; of a local government which is at once the dependent of and the scapegoat for central government and which enjoys little support either in Parliament or among the electorate; of security services which are protected from parliamentary scrutiny and which appear when the veil is briefly twitched aside to be barely under the control of ministers; of a police force which has appeared increasingly in a political role, which has little accountability, which has absorbed more and more resources while crime rates rise, and whose reputation for probity has been sadly dented.

For each of these ills there is a specific remedy: electoral reform, more powers for select committees and a reformed second chamber, freedom of information, the restructuring of local government (again) and devolution, a bill of rights or incorporation of the European Convention on Human Rights, and other proposals for the statutory protection of privacy, the control of the security services, the strengthening of employment rights and of anti-discrimination measures brought together in Labour's Charter of Rights. What has emerged over the last three or four years is a growing interest across the political spectrum in bringing these separate complaints together.

The major concern is the strength of an executive which exercises the prerogatives of the crown, subject to the political support and control of Parliament, with little recognition of the need for constitutional balance or constraints. Parliamentary supremacy has become a surrogate for popular sovereignty and is therefore confused with the supremacy of the House of Commons, which alone enjoys *legitimacy* because it is elected. The crown and the House of Lords are also part of Parliament, but the people play no part in their appointment and have never been asked whether or not these essential elements in the constitution enjoy their support. This support is taken for granted until some conflict between the different branches of government is threatened, when the supremacy of the House of Commons is asserted. This reflects a positivist or utilitarian interpretation of sovereignty: there must be a single locus of sovereignty and it must reflect the will of the majority. If we want to support the separation of powers, to guarantee individual rights against the majority, or to disperse powers among different levels of government, then we need some means for legitimating the necessary arrangements. If we do not have a written constitution, which can only be amended by special procedures, then any such arrangements are always at risk to narrow majorities in the House of Commons, which alone has any claim to represent the views of citizens.

Thus particular reforms may be important and interesting. But the essential question is whether the time has come to abandon incrementalism and to change the basis of the constitution. That is, to change from a single fundamental principle, the supremacy of Parliament, which is founded in custom and usage as recognized by the courts, to a fundamental law which is prior to, independent of and the source of authority for the system of government. A codification of existing practice and convention might be convenient, but it would not be enough. It is the peculiarity of our constitution not that it is not codified, but that the laws which make it up, whether statute, common or case law, have no special status. Parliament can make and unmake them as it chooses; a million British subjects can be deprived of their rights of abode by the same means that produce an alteration of the speed limit.

The much vaunted flexibility of the constitution suits nobody so much as an executive which has inherited a reservoir of prerogative powers and enjoys a dominant position in relation to the legislature and all other public authorities. In the past these features of the constitution, like the party system which exploits them, have been justified on the grounds that they help to provide firm and effective government. There is no doubt that single party government has advantages of cohesion, speed of response and clear locus of responsibility. It is less clear that it performs any better than other systems in the promotion of effective and acceptable public policies. There may be some truth in the view that there would be less concern about the constitution if the policies of successive British governments had been more successful. But there remains a constitutional case for reform: that the protection of individual rights, the decentralization of power within the United Kingdom and the United Kingdom's role in the development of the European Community would all be more readily and more satisfactorily realized within an explicitly constitutional framework.

Drafting concentrates the mind. It is for this reason that the Institute for Public Policy Research (IPPR) chose to produce the text of a constitution ('The Constitution of the United Kingdom', 1991) rather than another general discussion of the issues. The fact that we have gone to this trouble does not mean that we believe that the provisions of this constitution are the only or even the ideal answer. Although the proposal for a written constitution is in itself radical, much of the content is in the best (or worst) tradition of gradualism. The main features of the present constitution are left more or less intact: in particular the executive is drawn from the legislature, with all that entails for party government, the control of procedure, discipline and the purpose of elections. The supremacy of the constitution, however, entails a problem of a different order: a much greater constitutional role for the judiciary.

The involvement of the judiciary in what are seen as essentially political issues is probably the strongest ground of objection to a written constitution across the political spectrum. The problem is that while not all political questions are constitutional, all constitutional questions are inherently political. To separate off some questions and declare them fit for judicial interpretation and decision is an act of political will: of abnegation for politicians and of distrust of politicians on the part of the rest of us. We can leave aside aspersions on the character, opinions, social background and intellectual formation of lawyers. Politicians are imperfect and the process of election which gives them legitimacy also exposes them to immediate pressures from which the judges are to some extent protected. We need rules to govern the exercise of power. It is in the interest of the less powerful that those rules should be clear and explicit, to lessen their manipulation by the more powerful. We need rules that we can accept as fair in general, though we object to their application in particulars. We need rules to protect ourselves and others against ourselves. And we need referees, even bad referees, to interpret and enforce the rules.

The growing importance of European institutions in Britain's political and legal system give added weight to the case for constitutional protection. The United Kingdom is now the only member of the Council of Europe with no written constitution or enforceable bill of rights, our partners in Europe providing remedies for their citizens which are not available to UK citizens through the British courts. Moreover, the Westminster Parliament has accepted, through the Treaty of Rome and Single European Act 1986, the supremacy of European Community (EC) law. The British courts have become increasingly accustomed to interpreting domestic law in the light of EC law and, where necessary, overriding the domestic legislation. It is hardly defensible for Parliament to qualify its own sovereignty in commercial and employment matters while refusing to do so in matters such as human rights.

Any written constitution needs to incorporate some special procedures for its own amendment: without that the constitution has no special validity and is merely a codification of statutes. There are several reasons why a special procedure is needed. First, it gives the constitution the status which it needs as a fundamental document which is incapable of being altered at the whim of a temporary majority. Second, it enables fundamental human rights to be entrenched and incapable of being overridden by ordinary legislation. And third, in a federal constitution, power is shared between the central parliament and provincial parliaments. This means that the constitutional relationship between the state and its constituent nations and regions cannot be altered without the consent of both.

The supreme court in IPPR's constitution will have the power to make ordinary Acts of Parliament unconstitutional and hence play a much more powerful role in the constitution than the present House of Lords. As can be seen from the example of the United States, the power to appoint judges to courts with important constitutional powers can become a controversial political issue. If no changes were made to the present system of appointing judges, the temptation to depart from the recent tradition of impartiality in judicial appointments might become impossible to resist.

Judicial Independence

We have thus been obliged to give particular attention to the problem of judicial independence: it is no good relying on the judges for protection if they are in the pocket of the executive. The three essential features of judicial independence are:

1 freedom from political influence in the appointment of judges;
2 the protection of judges from undue political pressure while serving on the bench; and
3 protection from inproper removal from office.

We propose, first, that judges should be chosen by a judicial services commission. This is made all the more necessary by the replacement of the quasi-judicial office of Lord Chancellor with the office of Minister of Justice, a more overtly political minister who has no judicial function and will not have to be a qualified lawyer. There is nothing novel about the idea of a judicial services commission. Many Commonwealth countries have one. Where the present proposals differ is that the membership is not predominantly judicial or legal.

The constitution also provides protection for the independence of the judiciary by a better procedure and clear grounds for removal, and for protection against the judiciary by a new procedure for dealing with judicial misconduct under the judicial services commission.

The constitution contains a series of important reforms which should, first, make it more efficient by creating a Ministry of Justice to end the present irrational and damaging division of responsibility for the courts between the Home Office and the Lord Chancellor's Department; second, increase the independence of the judiciary by transferring responsibility for appointment and promotion to an independent judicial services commission; third, widen the background of the bench and make it more responsive to the feelings of litigants by including a powerful lay element in the judicial services commission and by creating a formal complaints procedure.

Local Government

The second major reason for wanting a written constitution rather than piecemeal reform is to deal with the centralization of power. The present policies towards local government are constitutional changes carried out by political means and could be reversed by the same means.

It will not therefore be enough to restore good relations and reform the structure and finances of local government. The reason is this: central government has and will always have a pressing interest in what local government is doing. There will always be pressure for central government to intervene to protect the economy, to maintain common standards, to rescue a local minority and so forth. Constitutional entrenchment of the powers of local government will not alter that. Nor is it possible to draw tidy lines of demarcation between the responsibilities of central and local government: there will always be a degree of overlap, of fusion and indeed confusion. In federal government much public policy is implemented through partnership, a word once used in this country also to describe the relations between central and local government. The difference is that in a federal constitution both central and local government have constitutional standing: local government has a base from which to negotiate. Here, local government is the creature of central government: it is whatever Parliament says it shall be, which is an invitation not only to continuous interference, but to occasional Whitehall engineering to reform local government structure, boundaries and functions to whatever the latest administrative fashion or party advantage dictates.

Devolution

We have also to consider central government itself and ask whether it needs to do all that it tries to do. There are two reasons for this. First, because central government is overloaded: Parliament groans under the burden of business which it cannot manage properly: the result is a mass of ill-digested legislation, inadequate scrutiny of government activity and failure to grapple with new responsibilities at the European level. The second reason is the need to accommodate the legitimate aspirations of the nations that make up the United Kingdom, while preserving the benefits of the union which we have painfully created over the last five hundred years. This need not and should not produce a conflict of loyalties. The question is: what is the appropriate way to give political expression to these overlapping identities?

Anybody who has taken the trouble to follow the lively debates in Scotland will be aware that there is a growing conviction that Scottish identity requires a more visible political expression in the way Scotland is governed. We have faced this question before and there was then strong opposition to the devolution proposals of the seventies, and with good reason. They were incoherent and inherently unstable: a reluctant damage-control operation with no constitutional backbone. We have a choice now between trying to treat Scotland as an exceptional case, a sort of autonomous region with special privileges which the Welsh and the Northern Irish will then demand as well; or using Scotland as a model for a general decentralization of government across the United Kingdom, by which we create not only an elected Scottish assembly to control the responsibilities of the Scottish Office, but similar assemblies for Wales, Northern Ireland and the regions of England. This would relieve Whitehall and Westminster of much domestic business and provide a tier of government to discharge responsibilities for transport, planning and the environment and economic development more effectively than either central or local government, as our European partners have found. The German Laender are of course the leading example, but France, Italy and Spain are rapidly developing their regional institutions. A project of this scale needs to have formal constitutional expression, for the same reasons as local government does. The balancing act between central, regional and local government requires each to have a firm base for negotiation and arrangements for revenue sharing and will of course require an independent arbitrator in the form of a constitutional court.

Is there a case for a grand design? It should be said at once that there are powerful arguments against doing anything more than is strictly and politically necessary. These apply with particular force to the proposals for England. Critics point to what they regard as the 'ignis fatuus' of reorganization: the notion that you can resolve or even address problems by institutional change. Local government is still reeling from the changes enforced on it over the last ten years. The last thing it needs is another upheaval. What is needed is a period of calm, of consolidation, a restoration of partnership between central and local government, based on agreed policies and adequate funding. It can be argued that there is nothing which a regional tier of government could do, which could not equally well be done by such cooperation. Sort out local government taxation, and concentrate on those areas of policy, like education and housing, which requires urgent attention. If you must make a bargain with the Scots, so be it. Otherwise constitutional change is a diversion, consuming time and political energy much better spent on the *real* business of government.

An alternative view is that, if the first step has to be taken, others will follow: and you might as well have a clear idea of where you are going and why. The constitutional changes proposed for Scotland are radical and in principle incompatible with current constitutional conventions. If they are enacted, with or without adjustments to the Union bargain, they will prove unstable and unacceptable either to Scotland or to the rest of the United Kingdom, particularly England.

The details of the scheme we have proposed are set out in the text of the constitution and discussed at length in the commentary. Apart from the obvious neglect of the special problems of Northern Ireland and the much less serious but equally intractable problem of the identity of the English regions, there are two features of the scheme which are likely to be controversial. The first is the way in which legislative power has been distributed between Parliament and the assemblies. This is an attempt to put into effect the principle of subsidiarity: the assemblies have rights to legislate on a broad range of domestic issues, but Parliament has concurrent powers to legislate where assembly legislation would be inadequate or have external effects. Parliament has exclusive legislative powers, but these in turn will effectively be shared with the European Community on the same basis. There are bound to be conflicts at both levels which if they cannot be resolved politically will have to be dealt with in the courts. The assemblies will at least be able to fight their corner, as indeed the UK government will need to do against the continual and unnecessary encroachment of detailed regulation from above.

The second controversial proposal is that for revenue sharing as a source of finance for the assemblies. This is an attempt to find a constitutional device to overcome the conundrum of regional and local government: how to find a tax base which provides a substantial proportion of local revenue and at the same time provides for the equalization of resources between richer and poorer areas. Tax-raising powers are commonly held to be essential to any genuine political independence, but if regional and local governments are left to their own resources there will be great inequalities in standards of public services between different areas. If on the other hand central government provides a substantial proportion of local resources in the form of equalization grants, it will inevitably become involved in prescribing the ways in which 'its money' is spent, and local autonomy or self-government will be undermined. This has proved the case even where redistribution has been carried through by elaborate formulae based on measurements of need. These do not remove the occasions for political judgement or the temptations to political manipulation. The suggestion here is to assign major tax revenues to the regions as of right with an entrenched formula for redistribution, while keeping the administration and control of the tax itself with central government.

There are many other specific innovations in the constitution which I cannot here discuss in detail. The detail is in any event far less important than the general argument that what is required is not piecemeal reform but a recasting of the constitutional mould. This reflects the underlying assumption that under the present constitution the executive is too powerful. Sceptics are apt to point out that despite the absence of entrenched rights the respect for civil liberties in Britain is as good as or better than in most other countries, whatever their constitutional arrangements; and, secondly, to observe that the over-mighty executive has proved remarkably ineffective in achieving its purposes, especially when confronted with well-established and well-organized interest groups. From one point of view the important failings of British governments have not been constitutional but political: the failure to modernize the economy and public services to match and progress of our international competitors. There is force in this observation. But the fact that governments are unsuccessful does not prevent them from being oppressive or diminish their ability to dictate the way in which decisions, however misguided or ineffective, are reached. Incompetent governments may be tyrannical and it is little comfort to the wrongly arrested, convicted or imprisoned to know that the government is unable to persuade the police or the legal profession to accept reform. The exaggerated majorities provided by the present electoral system reinforce the adversarial style of party politics, lead to a continuous emphasis on differences of policy rather than areas of agreement, to rapid changes of policy where stability and continuity are essential conditions of success, and to a failure to develop the consensus which would allow those conditions to be met. In effect the lack of the need to compromise, to reach agreement as a condition of getting things done, leads to the adoption of policies which do not command support and fail to be implemented. Constitutional reform, which is justified in its own terms, may also be a necessary condition for economic and social renewal.

2 The Liberal Democrat Written Constitution for the United Kingdom

John Macdonald QC

Power to the People

Liberal Democrats have long believed in the need for a new constitutional settlement. 'We the People', the Liberal Democrat green paper on constitutional reform, which was published in September 1990, broke new ground. We were the first UK party to advocate a written constitution and the first to say that the constitution should be drawn up by a constituent assembly elected by proportional representation. We said that the constitution would need the support of two-thirds of the constituent assembly and thus of two-thirds of the electorate. It is of the essence of any new constitutional settlement that it should have the widest possible support.

We must get rid of the doctrine of parliamentary sovereignty and start again. Liberal Democrats have an unshakeable belief in the sovereignty of the people. On the long march from an absolute monarchy we stopped, at the beginning of the twentieth century, at an elected dictatorship dominated by party whips. We must now take the last step to becoming a true democracy.

The content of a constitution is important, but we are also concerned in 'We the People' with how we get from here to there. We envisage a legislative programme lasting six years, spanning two Parliaments, culminating in the adoption of a written constitution which brings all the reforms together in a framework which is then entrenched. All the reforms interact. At the end of six years citizens will be able to discover the essentials of their government and their basic rights from a single document.

Essentials

The constitution must be short and easy to read. For Liberal Democrats the essentials of a written constitution are:

1 a federal constitution which divides power between different levels of government;
2 home rule for the nations and regions of the United Kingdom;
3 an enforceable bill of rights with equal access to the courts;
4 a supreme constitutional court;
5 a second chamber elected on a regional basis;
6 freedom of information;
7 a fair proportional voting system for all elections;
8 a democratic structure for Europe.

Changes to the Liberal Democrat Draft

The constitution which I drafted was published before the others considered by the Charter 88 convention. Having studied the Institute for Public Policy Research's (IPPR) draft, there are amendments which need to be made to mine. I mention four of them.

First, there is a need for a much sharper bill of rights. My draft simply incorporates the European Convention into UK law. The advantage of this is that the European Convention has already achieved very wide acceptance, but it is a very conservative document which gives governments too many escape clauses. A good example of this is the Lithgow case in which shareholders alleged a breach of Article 1 of the First Protocol to the Convention. Kincaid, a successful marine engineering company, was nationalized in 1977. It had cash reserves surplus to its requirements of £5 million which vested in the government. Two years later the shareholders were paid compensation amounting to £3.8 million. The government made a cash profit of £1.2 million and took a valuable business for nothing. The European Court of Human Rights held there was no breach of the convention. Nonsenses like this would be prevented by the IPPR draft, which is a great improvement on mine.

Second, the IPPR constitution expressly abolishes the royal prerogative. I think it is better to do this even though it will make the constitution longer because it will be necessary to give the government express power to act.

Third, the IPPR constitution defines the role of the queen as head of state. Again, I think it is better to deal with this specifically.

Fourth, while 'We the People' includes a Freedom of Information Act as one of its principal reforms, I did not refer to this in my draft. This was a mistake.

The Main differences Between the IPPR and Liberal Democrat Constitutions

Dawn Oliver, in her article in the April issue of *Parliamentary Affairs*,[1] notes that the constitutions are remarkable both for the areas in which there is consensus and for those in which there are divergencies of approach. I have indicated ways in which I think the common ground can be extended. Finally, I point to the two main differences where I think the Liberal Democrat draft is to be preferred.

First is the voting system. I have opted for the single transferable vote (STV), while the IPPR prefers a sophisticated version of the additional member system; either would be a great improvement on the present lottery. The IPPR report recalculates the 1987 result using their additional member system for a 500-member House of Commons. This gives the Conservatives 221 seats, Labour 156 and the Alliance 113. From a party political point of view I believe that the additional member system is likely to give the Liberal Democrats more seats than STV, but I do not support it. The great merit of STV is that it gives power to the voters and not to the parties. Under STV the voter can express a preference between men and women, black and white, wet and dry. STV will give us a House of Commons with more women and more members from the ethnic minorities.

The additional member system suffers from the disadvantage of giving the party machines too much power. STV too, contrary to the belief of many politicians and commentators, can provide a real link between the member of Parliament and communities. Five members of Parliament for Bristol have a much closer link with the city than if they each represent an arbitrary fifth of the area.

The second area where I think the Liberal Democrat proposals are more fully worked out than the IPPR ones is in the powers given to the nations and regions of the United Kingdom.

We would give home rule to Scotland, Wales, the regions of England and hopefully Northern Ireland. This means a massive transfer of power from Westminster and Whitehall to new economic and political centres in places as diverse as Edinburgh, Cardiff, Manchester, Bristol and Norwich. The UK Parliament would be smaller and confined to foreign affairs, defence, macroeconomic management and setting standards. Where functions of government are transferred to become the exclusive responsibility of nations and regions, Westminster and Whitehall would have no power to intervene.

Below regional governments will be one tier of principal local authorities – a core council. Below that there will be parish, town and community councils with increased powers. We will apply the subsidiarity principle from the European Commission right down to the parish council.

My constitution spells out the principles on which devolution of power will take place. The process will be driven from the grass roots. Many of the problems – such as whether an area should have a district council or a county council – will be solved locally. We look forward to the renaissance of local government with the independence of local councils guaranteed in the constitution.

The Task for Charter 88

The proposals contained in 'We the People' involve reforms which are as extensive as those carried through by the Asquith and Attlee governments of 1906 and 1945. A new constitutional settlement is urgently needed. It will only happen if those who believe in it capture the public imagination. Therein lies the challenge for Charter 88.

Notes

1 Dawn Oliver, 'Written constitutions: principles and problems', *Parliamentary Affairs*, 45 (1991), p. 151.

3 Constitutional Reform and Radical Change

Tony Benn MP and Andrew Hood

The recent constitutional debate has arisen in response to a growing recognition of the failings of British democracy. Our parliamentary tradition conceals the fact that immense powers of state – the crown prerogatives – are concentrated in the hands of the prime minister. By manipulating these powers, and in particular the extensive patronage they grant, the prime minister exercises a significant degree of personal control over the system of government.

In addition to the influence they give over the House of Commons, these crown powers allow the prime minister to make war, appoint and dismiss ministers, create peers, select archbishops and bishops, and sign international treaties without any constitutional obligation to consult Parliament. These powers are by to means insignificant: they have been used to establish a standing army of 20,000 American troops in 130 bases, over whom Parliament has no control; and more importantly they took Britain into the European Community with the consequence that today, for the first time since 1649, British ministers can enact laws by the simple exercise of the royal prerogative in the European Council of Ministers. Laws made here are then binding in British courts and Parliament cannot subsequently overturn them. The position described by Bagehot in *The English Constitution*[1] has effectively been reversed. Bagehot described the monarch as the 'dignified' element of the constitution, providing legitimacy to the disguised 'efficient' exercise of power by Parliament. Today it would be more accurate to describe the House of Commons as the dignified institution which is there to 'excite and preserve the reverence of the population'[2] while the powers of the crown, controlled by the prime minister, are the efficient part 'by which [the constitution], in fact, works and rules'.[3]

It is obviously not the case that any prime minister has ever, or could ever have, carte blanche to legislate according to his or her whim. The prime minister may have effective control over the prerogatives, but is still constrained by what is *politically acceptable* and the desire to preserve the confidence of Parliament and the markets. But the crux of the problem is not that there are no limits to the prime minister's power – the prime minister is quite clearly not a dictator – it is rather that the process by which this power is checked is profoundly undemocratic.

The prime minister is able to use the prerogatives, and in particular the powers of patronage, to create a distance between his or her own executive actions and the controlling influence of the Cabinet or the House of Commons. But isolated from the authority which a democratic 'mandate' in the Commons could give to the prime minister, he or she is unable to govern without the tacit support of the establishment (expressed crudely, this refers to the City, the security services, the crown, the European Community, the civil service and the military). The prime minister is thus compelled to make a series of compromises in order to retain the establishment's support and remain in power.

The question we need to address is how we can subject the royal prerogatives to democratic control; preferably including a devolution of crown powers to regional and local democratic accountability. This is a question which the mainstream of constitutional debate has tended to avoid. It has focused instead on the quite different question of how we can weaken the centralized control of the prerogatives. This, we are told, can be achieved by applying systems of checks and balances; by dividing, for example, the control of crown powers between the prime minister, the Cabinet, the judiciary and the European commissioners. To do this is essentially to tackle the problem of the centralized control of executive powers by placing them in the custody of unelected bodies. But this is the very problem inherent in our current arrangements. This solution may make prime ministers – and therefore governments – weaker, but will do very little to make them democratically accountable. Under these arrangements it will not be the British people, through the ballot box, who will gain control of crown powers and the right to judge the legitimacy of government actions, it is the establishment.

Measures which seek to limit the powers of government by rolling back the frontiers of the state will not necessarily make Britain more democratic. If, for example, you remove the government's ability to intervene in and control the economy, will you thereby increase the freedom of the unemployed and the homeless? Will those whose homes are being repossessed, or whose small businesses have collapsed, be saved by a reduction in the power of government? Far from liberating people, such moves will limit the ability of the government to protect people from oppressive and powerful forces in society such as big industrialists, the multinationals and the City of London. This approach to constitutional reform adopts a view of government as an administrator of the status quo, but ignores the potential for political institutions to act as a countervailing power to these undemocratic forces and to be a means by which people can resolve the problems which confront them.

Government structures should be the servants of the people, providing a mechanism by which they can pursue their own solutions to their own problems. The real issue, then, is the distribution and control of power. Constitutions are at heart political. But the constitutional reform debate is currently permeated by a search for an all-party consensus and the approval of the influential figures of the legal, political and media establishment. For this reason it must inevitably collapse into a strategy which is hostage to the demands of political 'realism' and thus the 'realities' of market forces, the European Community and the profit motive. To accept these specious realities is to condemn a large section of the population to continued unemployment, homelessness, economic insecurity, exploitation and prejudice.

Consensus-seeking reformers bracket such issues outside the constitutional debate. To seek to address social inequalities via constitutional reform is said to be naive and unrealistic. Such a lack of political vision is nothing new: when the suffragettes fought for the vote, when the African National Congress campaigned to overthrow apartheid, or when the Russians overthrew the recent military coup, their demands were greeted by those in power as unreasonable, impractical and flying in the face of reality. But in none of these cases did these groups tell their members to give in to political pragmatism. For the purpose was not to accommodate the existing consensus, but to be clear about their beliefs and to stand by them. The flaw in 'facing up to the harsh realities', in acknowledging that we are 'living in the real world', is that it entails doing exactly that – it accepts the prevailing reality when the object is to change it.

There is a tragedy in this, because a growing demand for change is being ignored. Demands for change are not immediately demands for democratic reform; rather, an interest in democracy is almost always secondary. People come up against particular problems, identify the cause and then confront their own inability to bring about a solution. It is at this point that the political system fails. When people cannot solve their problems or realize their aspirations they will inevitably come to see the political process as irrelevant. They will be forced to seek their own individual solutions. It is difficult to condemn people for buying their council houses when there is no collective alternative for securing high-quality housing. It is the fault of the left that it has failed to generate a workable, high-quality, collective solution: one which will convincingly meet people's needs and aspirations in a way which is more efficient than private and individual initiatives. Instead the leaders of all the main parties are in agreement. Everybody agrees on Europe, on America's domination of the United Nations, on privatization and trade union laws, and on the superiority of free markets. The Labour Party, recognizing a change in the form in which some people now seek to meet their aspirations – through home purchase as a means to gain secure housing, through the opportunity to make a windfall on privatization share issues as a means to short-term financial security – has mistaken this as a permanent acceptance of free market philosophy.

But it is quite wrong to believe that if people buy their own house they are in the same class as the Duke of Westminster; that if they own a few shares they have the same interests as Rupert Murdoch; or that if they run their own business they are in the same industrial league as ICI. The paradigm which suggests that we are all middle-class (except for a few who drop out into an underclass) forms the basis of the new consensus in British politics. As a result conventional politics has deteriorated to a series of non-events: to repeated personality clashes; to scandals and revelations which can only further the growing sense of cynicism.

Conventional politics is in a dual crisis: it fails adequately to control the powers of the executive, and, more crucially, parliamentary democracy itself is, in consequence, seen as increasingly irrelevant to the problems people face. The sense of pessimism, insecurity and anger is widespread and the unfocused desire for an alternative could, in its most extreme forms, expressing itself in rioting.

So a second question for constitutional reformers should be not only how we can repatriate crown powers to accountable democratic control, but how we can repatriate democracy itself in a way that is relevant to our own lives. How can we capture the means to control our futures, and help others who are trying to do the same, whether they live here or abroad?

Britain urgently needs a strong, powerful and sustained popular movement for democratic reform, to replace our rapidly decaying political institutions and to create a democratic, secular, federal commonwealth that would allow us to decide our own future. The Commonwealth of Britain Bill presented to the House of Commons in May 1991 provides the constitutional agenda for such a movement:

There would be an elected president, and a commonwealth parliament made up of a House of Commons and a House of the People.

There would also be national parliaments for England, Scotland and Wales, and a charter of rights (including social and economic rights and the right of women to reproductive choice).

Each constituency would be represented by one man and one woman and the voting age would be reduced to 16.

The commonwealth parliament would have powers over government, including the work of ministers representing Britain at the United Nations and in the European Communities, and would be required to approve the stationing of all foreign forces in Britain.

There would be a high court, and provision for the confirmation of judges and the election of magistrates.

Local authorities would acquire general powers, subject to statute.

The Church of England would be disestablished and religious freedom for all would be entrenched.

British jurisdiction over Northern Ireland would be terminated.

The constitutional status of the crown and the House of Lords would end, members of the royal family would enjoy all the rights of citizenship, including the right to stand for Parliament, and would receive pensions and accommodation.

There are four schedules setting out the text of the charter of rights, a new constitutional oath, the powers of local authorities, and providing for an annual report to Parliament by the security services.

Before its introduction the new constitution would have to be put to the electors in a national referendum, and a choice of the electoral system to be adopted would be included in that referendum.

Such a new constitutional settlement can only be built from the bottom up. In fact, every previous constitutional reform which has advanced democracy has been the product of pressure from below. Of course constitutional change can be imposed from above: the decision to abolish the Greater London Council, the extension of the Prevention of Terrorism Act, the Single European Act, the Maastricht Treaty and the trade union laws are a few examples. Such changes could only be made when the groups which might have opposed them were weak or divided, or, in the case of the unions, defeated. The suffragettes and the anti-apartheid campaigners won because they had a movement, not because they had cultivated friends in high places. To believe that the unelected commissioners in Brussels or the judiciary or members of Parliament will grant democratic rights is to misunderstand the nature of political change.

British democracy has degenerated into a spectator sport. We are expected to sit at home and observe. But democracy belongs in our homes and communities and places of work – it is not the preserve of pundits and polling organizations. Constitutional reform is part of the solution to the democratic deficit in Britain today, but it must give expression to people's aspirations for social, economic and political freedom. It must challenge the balance of power in society, not seek a rapprochement with the status quo. It is premature to suggest that history and politics have come to an end. All that is needed is that people should have confidence in themselves. Nothing can stop a determined movement from demanding justice.

Notes

1 Walter Bagehot, *The English Constitution*, ed. Richard Crossman (Fontana, London, 1963).
2 Ibid., p. 61.
3 Ibid.

4 A Free Market Approach to Constitutional Reform

Frank Vibert

Back to Principles

The 1980s witnessed a wide acceptance of market principles as the best organizing principles for economic activity. In the 1990s we are going to see a switch of attention to institutional and constitutional reform. Increasingly we will see constitutional processes and constitutional checks and balances as the best organizing principles for government.

It is sometimes asked why those who support the free market are interested in constitutional reform at all. One has only to look across at the United States, where supporters of the free market have long been at the forefront of constitutional debate. They recognize that government will always be tempted to encroach on areas of individual choice and freedom and to abuse its discretionary power, unless it is subject to well-defined rules, processes, checks and balances.

If we look at what underlay the revival of market processes in the 1970s and 1980s, clearly it owed much to a willingness to stress basic principles, to examine fundamental processes and incentives and to pursue market logic even if it meant challenging prevailing orthodoxies. A similar radical approach is needed in respect of constitutional and institutional reform.

If, therefore, we focus the debate on an examination of the principles, processes and incentive techniques needed to make government serve the people more effectively, what should these principles be?

Law and Contract

Supporters of the free market believe first of all in a greater role for law and contract. In this respect there is much common ground with other proposals for constitutional reform. Law and contract are a means to entrench individual rights against interference from government; they are mediating devices between the public and the private sectors and a constitutional tool for defining the different roles of different institutions.

One application of contract that is being carried forward in Britain is in respect of Whitehall. In this context, contract serves a dual purpose. It defines what government expects from a service; it defines, too, what service the consumer expects. By helping to distinguish the role of the civil servant in the provision of services from the role of the Civil Service in assisting government in its legislative duties, it also helps distinguish management and administration from policy formulation and advice. This approach to Whitehall still has some way to go in its implementation and one should not underestimate the changes it could bring.

By contrast we have neglected the role a constitutional framework can play in keeping institutions alive to their separate responsibilities and opportunities. If one considers how a more defined constitutional framework might help parliamentary institutions in Britain, an example is provided by the second chamber. Under our present arrangements the expertise in the second chamber is largely wasted. Most reformers agree that it should be an elected body in order to have legitimacy and so that the expertise represented in the second chamber can be brought to bear effectively. But should we look to a reformed second chamber simply to replicate its present function as a revising chamber? As such it is always likely to play a secondary role, be a pale shadow of the House of Commons or risk conflict with the House of Commons. Instead, we could look to a second chamber to perform rather different functions of scrutiny and investigation in areas where the House of Commons does not perform well. Its work on Europe might thus continue, but it might be able to play a larger role in respect of scrutiny over the British system of justice or over the many administrative and regulatory bodies that affect the lives of British citizens but are themselves arguably not sufficiently open to scrutiny.

Incentives and Institutional Behaviour

A second feature of the free market approach – and here it is in distinct contrast to some other approaches – is the focus on the incentives that influence the behaviour of institutions. One example is provided by the route to government office in the United Kingdom. Many members of Parliament go into the House of Commons with the ambition of ministerial office. Does this incentive in fact provide us with good ministers? Let us contrast the situation with that in the United States, where the president can call on talent wherever it may be – whether in Congress, in the Senate, in academic life or in business. We are unique in Europe in insisting on this indissoluble link between House of Commons membership and ministerial office, and need to question whether it always and in all cases serves us well.

Another example concerns the weakness of the House of Commons as an investigative body. Is there not an inherent conflict between the role of the House of Commons in providing support for the government and support for the government in waiting, and its role as an investigatory body? Are MPs really going to risk embarrassing their front benches by hard-hitting investigations?

These kinds of question about incentives lead in turn to a further set of questions about how one can tilt the balance of incentives so as to encourage bodies to work in a different fashion. For example, what would help bring about a more active scrutiny role by the House of Commons? Would such devices as term limitations for MPs be helpful in producing a more independent membership? Term limitations could also have a role in respect of an elected second chamber. Members would be elected there on party tickets, but if they had to serve a single term of perhaps six or seven years they could have considerable independence. And similarly one can ask incentive questions about the performance of the Civil Service. The Civil Service is still seen as a lifetime career. Does not this breed exactly the caricatured mandarin mentality that 'Whitehall knows best'?

Limiting the Discretionary Power of Governments

The third area of emphasis is on constitutional rules to limit the exercise of discretionary powers of government. This means limiting the encroachment of government not just on individuals but also, for example, on the media and other institutions important for a free society. It means looking at the scope for fiscal rules of a constitutional character to try and limit the bidding for votes through expenditure increases by governments in electoral difficulties. It also means looking at monetary constitutions as a way to limit the power of governments to devalue the currency. We should move towards an independent Bank of England with a constitutional or contractual duty to safeguard the currency.

Competing Approaches to Public Policy

Finally, the free market model stresses techniques for enlarging the scope of competing approaches to public policy. This embraces open processes when it comes to central government – including open budget processes, rather than the budgetary secrecy we have today. It could also involve the House of Commons going further into the processes of formulation of legislation, where Whitehall currently controls the consultative process. It means the reinvigoration of local government and resolving the triumvirate of form, finance and function for lower-level bodies.

Proportional Representation Is Not a Magic Key

Supporters of the free market believe there is no magic key to unlock constitutional reform, such as proportional representation. On the contrary, if we introduce proportional representation we have to accept the fact that it will bring coalition government in its train. Under our present system, coalitions are internalized within the two main parties. Under proportional representation, these coalitions could become externalized in the form of new parties. Coalition government strengthens the case for additional constitutional rules. They would be needed to safeguard against the over-fragmentation of party political processes; they would also be needed to guard against the abuse of powers by minorities in the formation of coalition governments. Budget deficits, and borrowing to tax future generations as a way of avoiding political choice in the present generation, are features of unstable coalition government, and there would also need to be rules against such behaviour.

The European Community

Supporters of the free market approach to government believe that in respect of the evolving constitution of the European Community, Britain cannot set up a Roman wall, or Maginot line, between domestic constitutional processes and the Community. Instead the focus should be on contributing to the principles and processes being built into Europe's future constitution, so that European political integration can be based on a decentralized approach and contain safeguards against overintrusion from Brussels.

We are offered three different approaches to achieving a decentralized Europe. One is what I would call a unilateral approach, a declaration of House of Commons supremacy or a declaration that UK constitutional law is superior law. This is the Roman wall or Maginot line approach. It is a false route because it denies the essence of constitutionalism, which is to resolve conflict through constitutional means and not through stand-offs. The second approach on offer is a 'Europe of the Regions'. This I also regard as a false path. A number of member states have difficulty in articulating their regional dimension. England is a case in point. But a more important aspect is that many regions will go to Brussels as supplicants looking for European structural grants and other forms of funding. Their relationship to Brussels will thus be a dependent relationship. A 'begging-bowl' approach is simply not the way to achieve competition between the nations of Europe. The third approach is to look for a wider variety of constitutional processes that can be enshrined in treaty form.

In Europe we desire a constitution which facilitates collective action where it is needed but at the same time guards against overcentralization and overintrusion. This means an emphasis on a careful definition of institutional roles, defences against centralizing behaviour, limits to the discretionary powers of Brussels, and justiciable rules in an appropriate judicial setting – not always that provided by the Court of Justice. These constitutional processes may contain elements of the other two approaches by, for example, setting limits to the jurisdiction of the European Court of Justice in relation to civil order questions, or by supplementing the prerogatives of national institutions by regional prerogatives where they have been articulated. But in any event they cannot be more than part of a much more thoroughgoing review of how to achieve decentralized arrangements in Europe.

A more constitutional approach to our own form of government will clearly help us play a more active role in building appropriate constitutional structures in Europe. The discretionary approach to government to which we have become accustomed in England does not serve as a model for Europe. We need to look for more formal checks and balances and to identify the incentives and motivation that influence institutional behaviour.

The Free Market Paradox

The free market approach is perhaps the most radical approach on offer in respect of the United Kingdom in terms of the kinds of question it asks. Yet at the same time it is highly conservative when it comes to Europe's constitutional future. This is because the limits on discretionary power which seem radical in a UK context also have to be incorporated into the European Community's constitutional future, and in that context they seem conservative. The paradox of radicalism in the United Kingdom and conservatism vis-à-vis Europe's constitutional future arises precisely because there is a consistent philosophical approach to constitutional reform in both settings. It is exactly this consistency of the free market approach that is needed in guiding both Europe's and Britain's constitutional future.

Part II

The Politics of Rights

5 A Bill of Rights for Britain

Anthony Lester QC

It is forty years since the Attlee Government wrestled with the idea of binding themselves and their successors to the European Convention on Human Rights. Hostile to the very idea of the convention, they only agreed to ratify it on the basis that UK citizens would never have recourse to the European Court of Human Rights against the United Kingdom. However, in 1966, the Wilson government, believing that few would ever bring a case against the United Kingdom, decided to allow men and women the right of individual petition to the European Commission and Court of Human Rights in Strasbourg.

Since then (leaving aside the many cases of delay in access to justice in Italy), the United Kingdom has been found in breach of convention rights more frequently than any other member state of the Council of Europe. In areas such as free speech, fair trial, personal privacy, prisoners' rights, sex and race equality, freedom from inhuman and degrading treatment or punishment, the United Kingdom has been found wanting; the list of violations is long and growing. Despite our dismal international record, successive governments, Labour and Conservative, have refused to incorporate the European Convention into UK law. Victims of human rights abuses too often have too take the long and expensive road to Strasbourg to secure justice, because Parliament has not authorized our courts to give remedies. And while the convention has been used to extend and protect some of our basic liberties in the face of increasingly authoritarian state power, the decisions of the judges of the European Court of Human Rights are often disappointingly narrow. Neither willing nor able to act as a substitute for a British constitutional court, they merely apply minimum standards, standards which UK law and practices fail miserably to match.

The government steadfastly refuses to do for the people of the United Kingdom what it has at last done for the people of Hong Kong in the Bill of Rights Ordinance of June 1991, namely to give them speedy and effective remedies in local courts for breaches of fundamental human rights and freedoms. (In this case it was the International Covenant on Civil and Political Rights which was incorporated into local law.) This means that the United Kingdom is now the only country in Europe or the democratic Commonwealth without an enforceable bill of rights. New Zealand, which was traditionally in the same position, enacted a bill of rights in 1990.

One of the fundamental principles of a democratic society is the rule of law, which means that an interference with individual rights should be subject to an effective check which should normally be assured by the judiciary – judicial control offering the best guarantees of independence, impartiality and a proper procedure.

The justification for the judicial protection of human rights is as follows. The protection of basic rights and freedoms cannot be left solely to law makers and civil servants. Parliament and local or regional authorities, as well as individual officials, may and do misuse their powers in the name of the majority, or simply through carelessness or thoughtlessness. It is the proper function of the independent courts in a true democracy to protect minorities against the tyranny of the majority, and against the misuse of public powers.

The rights and freedoms guaranteed by the European Convention and the International Covenant are too important to be subject to the whims of temporary majorities or to unnecessary interference by public officials. Without a bill of rights there is always the prospect of Parliament being pressured by populism to disenfranchise or handicap minorities. The most notorious case of this was the Commonwealth Immigrants Act 1968, where a Labour government stripped 200,000 East African Asians of their right to live in the only country of their citizenship. Needless to say their only recourse was to the European Convention.

Even if we had a more enlightened Parliament which was more sensitive to human rights, it would continue to delegate massively broad powers to public authorities. Other modern democracies recognize this, and alongside a bill of rights they have a code of administrative law to guide the judges in monitoring the use of these powers and administrators in exercising them.

Most breaches of civil rights and liberties in the United Kingdom do not occur because of the spite or ill-will of Parliament, government or civil servants. The pathology of human rights violations in this country involves uncontrolled administrative discretion. Public officials find that power is delightful, and absolute power absolutely delightful. For example, in the Sex Discrimination Act of 1975 and the Race Relations Act of 1976, Parliament gave wide discretionary powers to ministers to block proceedings in industrial tribunals on grounds of national security and deprive people of their right to access to justice. Similarly, the Home Secretary has wide powers to ban broadcasts on any grounds he or she sees fit and to regulate discipline in prisons.

Faced with this huge gap in the legal protection of human rights, British courts behave in what some would regard as an impeccably democratic manner – careful not to trample on parliamentary sovereignty, they give public authorities the benefit of the doubt, unless they behave so outrageously in defiance of logic or accepted moral standards as clearly to have taken leave of their senses. Except where European Community law can come to the rescue, or where there is specific UK human rights legislation, such as the anti-discrimination laws, British law is ethically aimless, uninformed by the general principles and standards guaranteed by the European Convention and by the International Covenant of Civil and Political Rights. There are no coherent standards to guide the judges when they interpret Acts of Parliament or develop the common law.

Unless and until Parliament gives them real guidance, British courts will not limit the powers of ministers or of public officials by using the European Convention as a bill of rights. This was made quite clear in the decision of the House of Lords in the broadcasting ban case (*R. v. Secretary of State for the Home Department, ex parte Brind*). The court said that they could not be expected to apply a stricter standard of necessity to the infringements of human rights (such as that laid down in the European Convention) when Parliament had specifically refrained from doing so.

To argue for a bill of rights is not to argue for a government of judges – perish the thought. It is to argue that the judicial branch of government should be given greater responsibility for remedying the misuse of public powers by either of the other two branches – the executive and legislature.

Public support for a bill of rights is strong. In a Mori poll, published in *The Independent* in October 1991, 79 per cent of respondents agreed that their rights would be most effectively protected if they were written down in a single document. When asked which bodies they felt they should be responsible for protecting a bill of rights, only 8 per cent of those questioned wanted a court with the kind of judges we have now. There was even less support for a reformed second chamber (7 per cent) to have this responsibility, and not much more for MPs in the House of Commons. The European Court of Human Rights in Strasbourg has rather more credibility, with 34 per cent of respondents saying that this body should continue to be responsible for guaranteeing basic rights. However, the majority opted for change: either courts made up of a more representative judiciary (40 per cent) or a new constitutional court with outside experts sitting alongside judges (29 per cent).

Of course, judges, like legislatures and civil servants, make mistakes. And like the European Court of Human Rights and most other European courts they are mainly male, white and middle-class. It is worrying that there is a lack of confidence in the British judicial record.

Much can be done to improve the training of the judiciary and ensure it is drawn from a wider social base, without compromising its independence from government. But public scepticism about the British judicial record should not be allowed to block urgently needed change. Where Parliament has done its job properly, for example in incorporating European Community law into national law, the British judicial record is impressive. The same is true of recent judicial achievement in developing administrative law independent of Parliament. If the Hong Kong example is anything to go by, a bill of rights has a positive, therapeutic effect upon the judiciary as well as upon other public authorities. In its first decision under the Bill of Rights Ordinance, the court of appeal ruled that presumptions of guilt in the Dangerous Drugs Ordinance were inconsistent with the bill of rights, stating that the bill should be interpreted in a broad and generous manner, having full regard to the relevance of international human rights norms.

Those who regard themselves as progressive and yet oppose judicial review of interference with fundamental rights and freedoms should reflect on the inevitable need for an enlightened judiciary to interpret specific human rights legislation. For example, our anti-discrimination legislation requires judges to make difficult decisions as to whether practices and procedures which hit disproportionately at women or ethnic minorities are objectively justifiable. This judicial task is similar to the task of the European Court of Human Rights in deciding whether interferences with basic rights and freedoms are necessary in a democratic society. British courts can and do give full faith to European

Community law where it protects fundamental freedoms such as the right to equal pay for work of equal value, equal treatment and freedom from sex discrimination.

Without being complacent, it should also be recognized that some of the judge-bashing indulged in by opponents of a bill of rights is prejudiced, ignorant and unfair.

The IPPR (Institute for Public Policy Research) model for a bill of rights, if implemented, would diminish the likelihood of narrow and illiberal judicial interpretation of a bill of rights. Under these proposals, exceptions to basic rights would be narrowly construed in favour of liberty, case law of the European courts would have to be followed by British courts, and people dissatisfied with UK judgements would continue to be able to have recourse to Strasbourg.

It is also essential that a bill of rights should be user friendly; that is to say, that special assistance should be available to allow individuals and groups of persons to bring their cases under the bill of rights. We need to establish a UK human rights commission with powers similar to those enjoyed by the Equal Opportunities Commission and the Commission for Racial Equality, though with rather more funding.

The need for a bill of rights will be all the greater if Scotland eventually has its own legislative assembly, so as to ensure minimum standards of citizenship throughout the United Kingdom – rights and freedoms to which one should be entitled irrespective of the territory in which one happens to live and work.

The time is over-ripe to translate the rights and freedoms to which we, the people of this country, are entitled under international law into our national legal system. Dicey wrote somewhere that it takes thirty years for an important idea to be realized under the rather lethargic British system. The proposal for a bill of rights was first mooted in November 1967. I hope that Dicey is right and that we will have this essential protection by 1997.

6 The Role of a Bill of Rights in a Democratic Constitution

Francesca Klug

The long philosophical dispute between those who see rights and liberties as most successfully secured through 'the silence of the law' (on both the left and right of the political spectrum) and those who favour legally enforceable rights is not necessarily replicated in the pro and anti camp on a bill of rights.[1] Liberty, for example, has long championed specific rights legislation whilst expressing concern about the role of the judges under a bill of rights. It is now firmly in support of a bill of rights based on the European Convention provided it is not judicially entrenched. Likewise there are a number of radical lawyers who are not opposed to legally enforceable rights per se, only to bills of rights which transfer law-making powers from an elected parliament to an unelected judiciary.[2]

Judicial Entrenchment

Protagonists and opponents alike tend to argue that a bill of rights *necessarily* involves the judges in having the *final* say on which Acts of Parliament do or do not comply with its terms. In practice, however, there are a number of possible approaches to enforcement. In New Zealand, for example, the attorney-general is the guardian of the 1990 Bill of Rights. Whilst this model stands accused of not being an entrenched bill at all, the 1982 Canadian Charter of Rights is entrenched and justiciable and yet allows Parliament (or a provincial legislature) expressly to override court decisions by passing acts 'notwithstanding' the provisions of the Charter. A similar opt-out clause was proposed by the Liberal Democrats in their 1990 draft constitution 'We, the People'. Others have suggested the use of a weaker device by which subsequent legislation would be interpreted consistently with a bill of rights *if at all possible*.[3]

Even the American constitution is ambiguous about the role of the courts in enforcing it.[4] It was not until 1803, in the case of *Marbury* v. *Madison*, that the doctrine of judicial review was first established. Until this century the Bill of Rights was rarely judicially enforced, and attempts to curb the power of the judges to strike down Acts of Congress continue to this day. For example, during the first two years of President Reagan's administration, 40 bills were introduced (but none passed) in Congress to strip the federal courts of their authority even to hear cases involving constitutional rights.[5]

There are two reasons why the issue of judicial entrenchment has attracted such attention. First, any bill of rights worthy of its name must be entrenched by one mechanism or another; that is, it must be a superior act to which all other legislation is supposed to conform and it must be difficult or impossible to amend or repeal. In a system like ours with no written constitution this is a departure from the doctrine of parliamentary sovereignty. According to this doctrine, the courts must give effect to an Act of Paliament whatever it says, and if Parliament changes its mind by a later act, the courts will give effect to that, as the most recent expression of the sovereign will. Of course British accession to the European Community (EC) has already dented this principle, with the judges giving priority to EC law where it proves inconsistent with domestic legislation.

Second, and just as important, a bill of rights is different from all other pieces of legislation in that it is a set of broad principles – some of which collide with each other – which are open to wide interpretation. Liberty's draft bill calls on the courts to pay due regard to the decisions and reports of international and regional human rights bodies in their rulings. However, none of the standard principles of statutory interpretation commonly employed by judges under the current British system – all of which rely on a degree of precision and detail in the act to be interpreted – can provide much guidance in the case of an open-textured bill of rights.

The combination of these two factors means that the body charged with entrenching the bill of rights effectively determines the law on civil and political rights. Examples from current practice illustrate this point. In Canada, the supreme court has overturned sexual offence reforms introduced in 1983 following pressure from women's groups, in particular the 'rape shield' provision which protected victims from questioning about their past sexual conduct. The judges ruled that this breached the fair trial provisions of the Charter. For a similar reason the 'absolute liability offence' of sex with a girl under the age of 14 has been amended to include a 'due diligence defence' for the accused. Judy Fudge, a Canadian legal academic, has observed that through these cases, 'another paradox of the Charter emerges; in the area of sexual assault legislation feminists may no longer be able to call upon the legislature to constrain the courts, whilst the legislature may be able to rely upon the courts to absolve itself of political responsibility'.[6] In cases of conflicting rights like these, there is inevitably a large measure of political or philosophical judgement involved in deciding where fundamental rights lie. This is why, in a democracy, there is a strong argument for such decisions remaining the responsibility of account- able, elected representatives.

The 1973 *Roe* v. *Wade* case, in which the US Supreme Court held that enforcement of state anti-abortion laws would unconstitutionally deprive women of their liberty, is an even more striking example of a bill of rights leading to judges substituting their views for those of elected politicians. The fact that the same women who oppose the Canadian decision would probably support the American one is irre- levant. As Archibald Cox, former solicitor general under Presidents Kennedy and Johnson and a committed supporter of the bill of rights, has said: 'As a legislator I would probably agree that the old laws against abortion should be radically changed. But I can find no evidence that warrants a court in saying that the basic values of our society as incorporated into our constitution dictates that choice.'[7] As the whittling away of abortion rights by the Bush Supreme Court demonstrated, a different set of judges appointed by a different political administration can come to the opposite view on abortion. Should a future Supreme Court rule that abortion (say, after the first trimester) breaches the bill of rights, the legislature would be power- less to intervene.

Liberty's Proposals for Democratic Entrenchment

When drawing up its draft bill of rights – 'The People's Charter', published in October 1991 – Liberty examined several different models of entrenchment. The approach Liberty adopted can best be summarized as judicial enforcement and democratic entrenchment. Based on the European Convention on Human Rights but broader in its scope, Liberty's draft bill is judicially enforced in the sense that individuals would be able to seek remedies for infringements of their rights through the courts. It is democratically entrenched in the sense that elected representatives would, in most cases, have the final say in determining which acts stand or fall under the bill of rights, provided special parliamentary procedures are invoked. At the same time the bill of rights could only be directly amended or repealed with the support of two-thirds of both Houses of Parliament. Rights legislation would still be determined through the democratic process but all laws – and the actions and decisions of public officials – would be subject to the bill of rights.

A version of the Canadian legislative override – referred to as a 'health warning' – is included in Liberty's model along with the stipulation that such acts have a maximum five-year lifespan. (In a proposal borrowed from the Labour Party's policy review, a reformed second chamber would have the power, should it choose to use it, to delay the coming into force for five years of any such 'health warning' legislation.) The Canadian legislative override has hardly ever been used. This is not surprising, given the political fallout and attendant publicity likely to befall any legislature that passes an act which carries an express acknowledgement – like a health warning on a cigarette pack – that it breaches the bill of rights.

The legislative override is in fact best viewed as an alternative to the derogation procedure in the European Convention on Human Rights (inserted at the behest of British government lawyers). The drawback to derogation is that it involves a tacit acceptance that human rights can be flouted during wars or public emergencies, precisely the circumstances which spurred the evolution of international or regional human rights instruments, like the Convention, in the first place. The legislative override, on the other hand, does not involve getting sanction – and hence legitimacy – for a breach of the bill of rights from the courts.

Given that it is effectively a form of derogation, it is easy to see why politicians are so unwilling to use the device of legislative override in the conflict of rights situations described above. Presumably neither the women's movement, nor their backers in the Canadian Parliament, wanted to reintroduce the 'rape shield' provision by acknowledging that it did not conform with the Charter of Rights. As a result the provision fell.

Liberty has proposed a novel mechanism to address such a scenario.

Suppose a new act was introduced to curb election expenditure by political parties at a national level. Under Liberty's proposals, should a newly created supreme court overturn such legislation as a breach of the right to freedom of expression – which is similar to what happened in Canada and the United States – this decision could, within a specified time limit, be referred by the courts, the government or a majority in Parliament to a special select committee called the Human Rights Scrutiny Committee (HRSC). (It must be emphasized that this would not apply where the courts outlawed subordinate legislation or administrative acts.) This committee would obviously not have any powers in itself but its decisions could affect subsequent parliamentary procedure.

There are, then, three possible outcomes. If two-thirds of the HRSC took the view that the hypothetical Election Expenditure Act was within the 'meaning, intention and spirit' of the bill of rights, Parliament could, by a resolution of both houses, attach a 'declaration of rights' to the legislation protecting it from further judicial (but not parliamentary) repeal. With such a formula the Canadian Parliament could have rescued its 'rape shield' and 'absolute liability' laws should it have wished to.

If, on the other hand, the Scrutiny Committee could not muster the requisite two-thirds majority then the court ruling would stand and the act would fall. If, finally, two-thirds of the HRSC considered that the act breached the bill of rights, it could only be re-enacted with a 'health warning' attached to it, and it would fall five years later.

Just as the European Convention sets aside certain articles which cannot be derogated from, so Liberty has proposed a distinction between those articles or clauses which involve a conflict of rights or are open to a wide variety of interpretations (the majority) and those which are much more clear cut and explicit. At the time of writing these include freedom of conscience, the right to be free from torture or slavery, and the right to vote and participate in public affairs. In these cases, judicial entrenchment would apply. (Following Liberty's consultation process, further Articles could well be added to this list when Liberty drafts its final bill.)

The composition and situation of the HRSC are vital if the committee is not to suffer from the executive domination which befalls the usual operation of the legislature under the British constitution. On the assumption that the bill of rights is introduced as part of a wider constitutional settlement, the HRSC would be based in a reformed second chamber which would be elected on a proportional basis. The chair would either be elected by the committee or would automatically be occupied by the largest opposition party (as per the Public Accounts Committee). The HRSC would be consulted on legislation prior to enactment, but its decisions could only affect parliamentary procedure along the lines described above following a court ruling on an Act of Parliament.

In all of its decisions this committee would be advised by a human rights commission, an appointed body composed of lawyers (academics and practitioners), human rights non-governmental organizations, and lay individuals with knowledge and/or experience of human rights abuse. In advising the HRSC, the commission would be required to draw upon international human rights jurisprudence. Its advice would be public and published, acting as a counter to any pressures placed on HRSC members by the whips.

Recourse to the European Commission of Human Rights would still be available in the unlikely event that the HRSC flouted the bill of rights for political ends. Judicial review would likewise be possible if HRSC decisions appeared to weaken rights rather than operate within the 'meaning, intention and spirit' of the bill.

A Critique of Democratic Entrenchment

There are three major criticisms that can be levelled at Liberty's proposals. First, that they blur the separation of powers that any new constitutional settlement would be designed to extend. Second, that they do not provide sufficient protection for minority rights against the effects of a majoritarian democracy. Third, that they do not 'entrench' rights, which is the whole purpose of a bill of rights.

So far as the question of the separation of powers is concerned, the classic conceptual distinction is between law making, law executing and law adjudicating.[8] Under the unwritten constitution of the United Kingdom there is, in practice, a considerable overlap in these powers. The need to address this confusion has provided one of the spurs behind demands for constitutional reform. However, the 'broad-brush' approach of any bill of rights means, as we have seen, that the role of interpretation or adjudication blurs with the role of law making to a greater extent than it already does under ordinary statutes. If Liberty's model stands accused of conferring a law-adjudicating function on the Human Rights Scrutiny Committee (which is rather like the function of the Committee of Ministers under the European Convention on Human Rights), the judicially entrenched model is equally in the dock for increasing the legislative function of the judiciary. As Reed Dickson has argued in his major book, *The Interpretation and Application of Statutes*, 'the greater the range of choices open to the judge, the greater his law-making as opposed to his law-finding function. If the statute is a bill of rights with broad, open-textured provisions, the scope for judicial legislation will be vast.'[9]

Law making by judicial rulings (common law) is already widespread. It is ironic that judicial entrenchment of a bill of rights would effectively widen the scope of judges' law when written constitutions are partially aimed at clarifying the law through statute. This is notwithstanding the fact that the common law would itself be bound by the bill of rights. Ferdinand Mount recognized this point when he wrote: 'The familiar argument that incorporation (of the European Convention) would diminish the relative importance of English common law seems to me precisely the reverse of the truth.'[10] If, for the first time, we were to gain privacy rights through incorporating the European Convention into UK law, for example, it would be for the judges to determine how this should balance with our new right to freedom of expression. They would also have to decide what limitations on privacy are 'necessary in a democratic society' in the interests of, amongst other things, 'national security,' 'the economic well-being of the country' and 'the protection of morals.'[11]

Legislation introduced to give substance to such broad rights would be subject to judicial approval. If, for example, the courts ruled that a statutory right of reply to newspaper articles breached the right to freedom of expression the law would fall. The significant point is that under a judicially entrenched model, and unlike now, Parliament would be powerless to alter the effects of such judicial decisions except through a constitutional amendment (which is deliberately difficult to achieve).

The thrust of the argument against judicial entrenchment of a bill of rights does not, in my view, apply to judicial entrenchment of written constitutions. The comprehensive constitution drafted by the Institute for Public Policy Research argues for judicial entrenchment on the ground that 'representative government cannot work fairly or at all without certain agreed prior conditions or "rules of the game".'[12] To be the adjudicator of a written constitution which establishes such rules –

including the means of enforcing a bill of rights – is a logical extension of the judicial role and therefore does not breach the principle of the separation of powers. However, this is quite different from having the final say in determining how the rights and liberties of the people are established in law.

The issue of minority rights dates back to the vision for a bill of rights held by American constitutional reformer James Madison. He saw its major role as one of protector of individuals and minorities against popular majorities. The fact that the original American constitution omitted to give any political rights to women and counted slaves as two-thirds of all other persons seems to have escaped his notice.[13] Indeed, in 1857, in *Dred Scott* v. *Sandford*, the supreme court held that national citizenship could not extend to a freed slave and that the constitution prevented Congress from abolishing slavery. The 1896 case of *Plessy* v. *Ferguson* confirmed that racial segregation was legal. Although the famous anti-segregation decision in 1954, *Brown* v. *Board of Education*, had a dramatic effect in turning the tide against legalized discrimination and in favour of affirmative action in recent years, the American Civil Liberties Union has increasingly been forced to turn to the legislature to protect minority rights from the judgements of the courts.

In the United Kingdom, the main legal protections of minorities, such as they are, have come from Parliament, with the courts presenting a mixed record in applying them. Even under the European Convention – which only guarantees equality in the exercise of the rights it upholds – some minorities have fared better than others. Gays, prisoners and people with mental illness have all benefited; transsexuals, refugees and migrants have had mixed results.[14]

The point of these illustrations is that the judges cannot be assumed to protect minorities any more than Parliament can. It is the bill of rights they can be assumed to protect. In so doing they will come up against a variety of interpretations – subject to significant changes over time – about which minorities and which rights are covered by its broad terms.

In the checks and balances created by Liberty's democratic entrenchment procedure, there are a number of safeguards against the 'will of the majority' riding roughshod over the minority. These include the significant role of the Human Rights Commission which, in addition to minority group members, would be composed of specialists steeped in international human rights law. Through the operation of the HRSC, fundamental rights legislation would no longer be subject to the same parliamentary procedures as laws covering dog registration. Moreover, the courts would still have a major role in enforcing the bill of rights. They would be charged with ensuring that executive actions (and subordinate legislation) complied with the bill, which, on the basis of the American experience, would form most of the litigation under the bill of rights. The supreme court could also repeal Acts of Parliament which could only be re-enacted with a 'health warning' or 'declaration of rights' attached to them. In all such cases the judges' view would obviously be a significant additional pressure on the ultimate course the legislature decided to take.

Finally on the question of entrenchment, the evidence presented here demonstrates that judicial entrenchment can no more entrench or safeguard rights, in any absolute sense, than democratic entrenchment can. What both models can do is provide stronger safeguards than our current system of common law rights and ordinary legislation is ever likely to.

Conclusion

The case for a bill of rights is overwhelming. It would provide us with a clutch of positive rights overnight, ending our reliance on common-law freedoms which sets us apart from nearly all modern democracies. In its statement of general principles, it would protect us from future breaches of fundamental rights which cannot be fully predicted in ordinary legislation. It would empower individuals by enabling them to take public officials, including the government, to court for infringing their liberties.

However, the debate about the best means of entrenching such a bill raises real concerns for all democrats, which should not simply be ignored. The model proposed by Liberty meets the three basic requirements of a bill of rights. It is justiciable, it is superior legislation which can only be amended through extraordinary parliamentary majorities, and the decisions and actions of all branches of the state are subject to its terms. However, the power to legislate to determine which rights prevail when they collide with each other – a judgement which is bound to alter over time and under different circumstances – ultimately remains with the legislature. Above all, Liberty's approach takes us back to the original intent of the eighteenth-century framers of bills of rights, whose basic concern was to set down in statute the fundamental rights of the people vis-à-vis their rulers. It could not have been their intention to create the kind of dynastic arrangements found in some twentieth-century democracies in which supreme court judges generally have to die or retire before the interpretation of the conflicting principles enshrined in a bill of rights can be reviewed.

One of the most crucial elements in Liberty's model is the role it gives to civil society. Feminist critics of the effects of the Canadian Charter argue that the discourse about rights has been removed from the political to the judicial sphere, making it remote and inaccessible to the bulk of ordinary people. A recent opinion poll in the United States revealed that, after two hundred years, only one in three citizens are familiar with the bill of rights. Under Liberty's proposals, in addition to the right of individuals to take cases under the bill through the courts, there would be lay involvement in the Human Rights Commission, and the public scrutiny likely to attach to 'health warning' or 'declaration of rights' acts could well galvanize the different groups involved to make their voices heard (minorities as well as majorities). Furthermore, in recognition of the fact that the source of legitimacy of a bill of rights ultimately lies with the people, Liberty proposes that its introduction should be subject to a national referendum.

In the final analysis, there is no substitute for the role of eternal vigilance in entrenching fundamental rights. As the famous US federal court judge, Learned Hand, once said 'Liberty lies in the hearts of men and women; when it dies there, no constitution, no law, no court can save it.'[15]

Notes

This chapter was written with research assistance from Suzanne Gee.

1 For an interesting discussion of these positions see A. Ryan, 'The British, the American and rights', in *A Culture of Rights: The Bill of Rights in Philosophy, Politics and Law, 1791 and 1991*, eds M. Lacey and K. Haakonssen (Cambridge University Press, New York, 1991).

2 See, for example, K.D. Ewing and C.A. Gearty, *Democracy or a Bill of Rights* (Society of Labour Lawyers, 1991).

3 For example, the 1986 Human Rights Bill introduced by Sir Edward Gardiner MP and the 1990 Human Rights Bill introduced by Graham Allen MP.

4   See Article iii, Section 2, of the American constitution: 'The Judicial power shall extend to all Cases, in Law and Equity, arising under this Constitution . . . with such Exceptions and Under such Regulations as the Congress shall make.'

5   I. Glasser, *Visions of Liberty* (Arcade Publishing, New York, 1991), p. 52.

6   Judy Fudge 'The effect of entrenching a bill of rights upon political discourse; feminist demands and sexual violence in Canada', *International Journal of the Sociology of Law*, 17 (1989), pp. 445–63. She cites other sexual offence legislation protecting women overturned by charter rulings.

7   A. Cox 'Storm over the Supreme Court,' in *The Evolving Constitution; Essays on the Bill of Rights and the US Supreme Court*, ed. Norman Dawson (Wesleyan University Press, 1987), p. 20.

8   E.C.S. Wade and A.W. Bradley, *Constitutional and Administrative Law* (Longman, Harlow, 1985), p. 59.

9   Quoted in Michael Zander, *The Law Making Process* (Weidenfeld and Nicolson, London, 1989), p. 177. See also J. Oakes, 'The proper role of the federal courts in enforcing the Bill of Rights', in Cox, *Evolving Constitution*, p. 181.

10   Ferdinand Mount, *The British Constitution Now* (Heinemann, London, 1992), p. 232.

11   European Convention on Human Rights, Article 8(2).

12   *The Constitution of the United Kingdom* (IPPR, London, 1991), p. 12.

13   The American Constitution, Article i, Section 2.

14   Transsexuals had not been able to obtain the right to have their birth certificate altered until the 1992 case of *B.* v. *France*. With the notable exception of *Beldjoudi* v. *France* (26.3.92), the European Court has rarely been prepared to rule against states in deportation, extradition or expulsion cases. For a summary of recent developments in European Convention law see John Wadham, 'Recent developments in European Convention law', *Legal Action*, 7 (1992), pp. 11–14.

15   Quoted by Oakes, 'The proper role', p. 178.

7 Welfare Rights and the Constitution

Ruth Lister

Should social and economic rights underpin our civil and political freedoms? The answer has to be 'yes', if the agenda for constitutional reform is to be made more relevant to the poor and the powerless.

The agenda for constitutional reform must incorporate social and economic rights because our ability to exercise our civil and political freedoms is in part a function of our social and economic position. It is not possible to consider substantive, as opposed to formal, civil and political rights in isolation from inequalities of class, 'race' and gender, or from the ways in which poverty or, say, society's attitudes towards disability exclude people from full civil and political citizenship.

The rights enshrined in Charter 88 therefore need to be underpinned by a firm web of social and economic rights, if they are to be meaningful for those in poverty and without power. Such rights are especially important in the construction of women's citizenship because of women's greater vulnerability to poverty and their particular relationship to the welfare and political systems.[1]

Research evidence drawn upon by the Speaker's Commission[2] and, more recently, from a MORI poll[3] commissioned by the Joseph Rowntree Reform Trust indicates that the majority sees social rights as central to what citizenship and a bill of rights should be about.

The argument, commonly voiced, that citizenship cannot embrace social and economic rights because they are categorically different from civil and political rights has been countered vigorously by Raymond Plant, most recently as part of an Institute for Public Policy Research (IPPR) project on social rights. He argues that the problems attributed by critics to the enforcement of social and economic rights apply equally to civil and political rights; in particular, both imply a claim on resources. Plant suggests that 'the idea of social and economic rights' can provide a philosophical rationale for the various citizens' charters on offer from the political parties and 'can link charters of social rights to a Bill of Rights to protect civil and political rights, so as to make them independent but parallel and mutually reinforcing ways of empowering citizens.'[4]

In this chapter, I discuss briefly how these links might be made, with particular reference to rights to income maintenance, drawing on a charter for social citizenship which I have outlined elsewhere,[5] as well as on the IPPR social rights project. The charter should be taken as indicative rather than as written in tablets of stone. Moreover, it is confined to rights within this particular state, yet ultimately such rights will need to be considered in a more international, and certainly a European, context. As a number of contributors to a recent volume on citizenship have argued, 'an interdependent world may be creating complex systems of rights and duties which entail breaches of existing frontiers'.[6]

The proposed charter is founded on the following broad principle: the wages, social security and tax systems should, together, ensure that all members of society have sufficient income to enable them to meet their public and private obligations as citizens and to exercise effectively their legal, political and social rights as citizens. Broadly, the charter then covers:

rights to income from employment and access to employment;
a range of principles for social security which embrace:
(a) social security as a right, not subject to discretion or charity;
(b) benefit levels sufficient to enable participation as citizens;
(c) entitlement to social security, moving away from means and contribution
     tests and towards individual entitlement, thereby giving more women
     independent access to benefits;
(d) delivery of a first-class service which ensures equal access and treatment
     and the eradication of racism;
the specific rights of children, disabled people and immigrants;
access to information, advice and assistance to enable people to enforce these
and other welfare rights.

Could such rights be enforced by constitutional means? To answer this question, we need to distinguish between different levels of rights.

Three such levels might be identified. The boundaries between them are potentially fluid and it is conceivable that the first and second levels could be amalgamated.

First, there is the level of broad principle, which can be incorporated into a constitution and which has been in a number of countries. For example, Article 3 of the Italian Constitution states:

It is the task of the Republic to remove all obstacles of an economic and social nature, which, by limiting the freedom and equality of citizens, prevent the full development of the individual and the participation of all workers in the political, economic and social organisation of the country.

Lord Scarman has quoted the example of the Indian Constitution, where the social and economic rights set out are not directly enforceable in the courts but are to be borne in mind and respected by all institutions of government.[7]

The incorporation of such broad principles at the constitutional level is no panacea, leading automatically to tangible social and economic rights. It would, nevertheless, provide a touchstone by which provisions could be tested. Similarly, it could strengthen the position of those struggling to improve and extend social and economic rights or to defend existing ones from attack.

The second level would elaborate on the broad principles in a more detailed statement of policy objectives. This would be something akin to John Major's Citizen's Charter, except that it would be a genuine citizen's charter rather than a consumer's charter masquerading as one. An attempt to draw up such a charter has been made by Norman Lewis and Mary Seneviratne.[8] As Lewis and Seneviratne point out, the United Kingdom is already a party to international treaties and conventions which seek to guarantee social rights as part of the international law of human rights. The most important of these, they suggest, is the European Social Charter (ESC) of the Council of Europe, which was adopted in 1961 and came into force in 1965.

The ESC was promulgated to complement the European Convention on Human Rights in order to progress the social and economic aspects of the UN Declaration of Human Rights. The ESC and the Human Rights Convention together were seen as 'the buttress upholding the fundamental rights of the individual. While the European Convention on Human Rights is principally aimed at protecting civil and political rights, the ESC seeks to protect rights in the social and economic sphere'.[9] Yet the ESC is virtually unknown in this country.

Lewis and Seneviratne have based their own proposed social charter on the main articles of the ESC, with a number of amendments and additions. The aims embodied in the preamble echo and extend those of the ESC: the improvement in the living standards and promotion of the social well-being of all citizens; the highest standards of health and social welfare and the right to self-fulfilment and expression; the enjoyment of social rights without discrimination. As such, they resemble the kind of general principles that, it has been argued above, can be enunciated within a constitution. They also stand firmly in the tradition of T.H. Marshall who defined the social element of citizenship as: 'the whole range from the right to a modicum of economic welfare and security to the right to share to the full in the social heritage and to live the life of a civilised being, according to the standard prevailing in the society'.[10]

The charter then outlines a series of rights to: protection of health; medical care; social security; social and medical assistance; benefit from social welfare services; vocational guidance and training; old-age benefits; and housing; plus specific rights for disabled people, older people, families and mothers and children. An anti-poverty provision is explicitly excluded, but it is accepted that consideration should be given to such a provision at a later stage.

The charter would be an Act of Parliament in the light of which new and existing pieces of social legislation would then be interpreted. It would not, itself, be entrenched initially. However, the authors leave open the question of whether it might ultimately be so in the context of a written constitution. They also emphasize that, in the absence of entrenchment, its special status should be recognized and protected by means of a special standing advisory committee.

The rights the Charter details are not, in fact, couched in the language of rights residing in individuals but in that of duties pertaining to government. As such, they would have to be backed up by resources and by more specific legislation which did provide such rights. This brings us to the third level of a social rights strategy, namely enforceable rights set out in legislation and backed up by an independent appeal system and ultimately the courts.

Specific laws can provide rights to specific benefits and services, although rights to the latter are more difficult to enforce than to the former. Laws can also provide negative protective rights. Particularly important here is anti-discrimination legislation. The lack of such leg-islation to protect the rights of disabled people is now a central focus of disability politics. It is argued that a law prohibiting discrimination on grounds of disability is the one single most important measure needed to enhance the citizenship of disabled people.[11] A model has been provided by the achievement of such legislation by the disability rights movement in the United States. Other forms of discrimination which could be outlawed by legislation include those on grounds of age or sexual orientation.

Enforcement of anti-discrimination legislation is relatively straight-forward, as is that of the substance of specific rights to income main-tenance. It is rather more difficult to enforce rights to decent service delivery, although it is possible, for example, to envisage an enforce-able right to have a social security claim dealt with in a specified time period. If claimants were given a bonus when a claim was not met within a specified target time, there would be a very real incentive to meet such targets. However, there would then be a danger, already identified in the reports of the chief adjudication officer, that a preoccu-pation with swift delivery of benefits could be at the expense of accu-rate assessment of entitlement. Errors in benefit paid are less visible to the claimant than delays in payment, and can go undetected without the intervention of someone with welfare rights expertise.

This underlines the importance of a comprehensive network of ad-vice and advocacy agencies to ensure that enforceability of rights does not remain a theoretical concept. The National Consumer Council has referred to access to information and advice as 'the fourth right of citizenship' (the title of one of its publications in 1977), and more recently the National Council of Voluntary Organizations has stressed the importance of such networks as part of the 'infrastructure of citi-zenship'. Despite the legal aid and advice schemes and the expansion of the number of advice agencies, large numbers of people in poverty – those most in need of strong social rights – still do not have access to the kind of advice and assistance they need to make a reality of their social and legal rights. Moreover, cutbacks mean that such access is now worsening rather than improving.

Access to information, advice and advocacy is an important element in the establishment of procedural rights, which are explored in some depth in relation to health and welfare services in the IPPR social rights project. Procedural rights to welfare focus on the way in which people are treated and in which decisions are taken; as such they constitute 'a hybrid between civil and social rights'.[12] Their importance is stressed by Denis Galligan, who asserts that: 'it is part of the very idea of a substantive right that procedures be available to secure it. In welfare this means that where there are rights to certain benefits, there are procedural rights to the means necessary to obtain these benefits.'[13] Procedural rights are also, he points out, about the right to be treated with dignity and respect, another important element in what it means to be a citizen – in the broadest sense of the word, including those who are not technically citizens under our citizenship laws.

It is easier to establish and enforce procedural rights than substantive rights in the area of welfare services. Other contributors to the IPPR report suggest ways in which procedural rights could be developed in the fields of health and community care and social work. A number of such rights have already been codified in the Disabled Persons Act 1986, but they are not now to be implemented. Legislation does, however, place clear duties on local authorities to assess the needs of disabled people for certain services. Where such a need has been established, the legislation is now being used in some places to require the authority to provide the service. Although the legislation has weaknesses and there is considerable confusion as to what duties, and thereby implied rights, it contains, it does provide an example of how a substantive right to a service can be embodied in a legislative duty to provide it. The problem, as with any right of this kind, is when it comes into collision with budget constraints and consequent rationing of services.

As IPPR suggests, this points to a pragmatic approach to the development of welfare rights rather than a search for universal solutions: 'the most productive way of introducing rights into welfare is likely to be piecemeal and experimental, but within the context of a shared set of values'.[14]

Plant argues for looking at ways in which enforceable social rights can be introduced on a case-by-case basis. Such an approach, he contends, would provide a new philosophy of the public sector and a new approach to empowerment, which he contrasts with approaches based on the market on the one hand and on regulation or democratic accountability on the other.

Ultimately, however, social citizenship needs to embody both clear social rights and democratic accountability. Both substantive and procedural rights are more likely to address people's needs if service users have been involved in their development. Moreover, such an approach incorporates a more dynamic and active conception of citizenship than one based simply on treating people as the passive recipients of rights. The difficulties, especially in relation to nationally determined rights such as exist in the sphere of income maintenance, are not to be underestimated. These difficulties are magnified in the case of those traditionally marginalized in the political sphere, whose voices can be drowned out by those of more powerful groups.[15]

In conclusion, the transformation of subjects into citizens cannot be achieved without addressing the sphere of social and economic as well as civil and political rights. A democratic constitution can and should provide the framework in which such rights can be established. More specific legislation can then translate the broad constitutional principles into enforceable rights, although this is easier to achieve in some areas of welfare than others. If the constitutional debate ignores these questions, it will be in danger of becoming an irrelevance to marginalized groups, such as those in poverty, many women and black people, and disabled people. So long as their civil and political rights are undermined by their lack of effective social and economic rights, their status as citizens will be profoundly compromised.

Notes

1   R. Lister, 'Women, economic dependency and citizenship', *Journal of Social Policy*, 19 (1990), pp. 445–67.

2   Speaker's Commission on Citizenship, *Encouraging Citizenship* (HMSO, London, 1990).

3   P. Dunleavy and S. Weir, 'They want to see it in writing', *The Independent*, 2 October 1991.

4   R. Plant, 'Citizenship, rights and welfare', in A. Coote (ed.), *The Welfare of Citizens* (Institute of Public Policy Research/Rivers Oram Press, London, 1992), p. 17.

5   R. Lister, *The Exclusive Society: Citizenship and the Poor* (CPAG, London, 1990).

6   G. Perry, 'Paths to citizenship', in *The Frontiers of Citizenship*, ed. U. Vogel and M. Moran (Macmillan, Basingstoke, 1991), p. 166.

7   Interview with Lord Scarman, *New Statesman and Society*, 28 September 1990.

8   N. Lewis and M. Seneviratne, 'A social charter for Britain', in Coote, *The Welfare of Citizens*.

9 Ibid., p. 32.

10 T.H. Marshall, *Citizenship and Social Class* (Cambridge University Press, Cambridge, 1952), p. 11.

11 See, for instance, I. Bynoe, M. Oliver and C. Barnes, *Equal Rights for Disabled People*, (IPPR, London, 1991).

12 Coote, *The Welfare of Citizens*, p. 9.

13 D. Galligan, 'Procedural rights in social welfare', in Coote, *The Welfare of Citizens*, p. 64.

14 Coote, *The Welfare of Citizens*, p. 10.

15 See S. Croft and P. Beresford, *From Paternalism to Participation* (Open Services Project/Joseph Rowntree Foundation, London, 1990).

As Marina Warner points out in the concluding chapter to this book, the polis has a social face which is cultural and spiritual. The freedom of individuals (male, in effect, despite universalistic language) to act as citizens has always been linked in the history of ideas to their capacity to maintain a life of the mind and the spirit, a life that is stunted when there is impoverishment. Sometimes, this has been thought to imply that the poor be excluded from politics; sometimes, that society's resources be redistributed so as to reduce the constraint of poverty upon human agency. Women have traditionally been excluded from the polis because our 'natural' role is supposedly that of wife and mother. This has been compounded by the belief that if we are allowed into the public sphere, our 'natural', domestic capacities fit us only for low-paid, low-status occupations.

In Scandinavian countries, the public maintenance of incomes, the provision of services (intended originally to engender social cohesion between economic classes) and sex equality laws have reinforced one another, enabling women to act more fully as political citizens. But, during the last 12 years in the United Kingdom, the dominant public philosophy has been inimical to such policies. The opposition among political leaders to social policy at home and in Europe, combined with antagonism to constitutional reform, has a mirror image in the findings reported at the Manchester convention by Patrick Dunleavy. He points out that surveys show that people who favour a new domestic constitutional settlement also tend to support European integration and the reconstruction of the welfare state, albeit in a new form which acknowledges a human need for autonomy. It may be that those who regret incursions on the domestic welfare state view the EC with hope, as a means of resuscitating a sense of communality. Advocates of legal rights to sex equality see the Community, though imperfect, as an avenue for maintaining provisions or making them more enforceable.

In our convention workshop on women's legal and constitutional rights, Elaine Donnelly pointed out that the absence of a constitution in the United Kingdom makes it more difficult to ensure equal rights for women. In fields that are covered by the Treaty of Rome, however, the EC does do something like this. It provides a framework for the European Court of Justice (ECJ) to judge national laws and practices. The Treaty of Rome calls for equal pay for work of equal value, equal treatment in other conditions of employment, equal treatment in state social security schemes, equal treatment in private occupational pension schemes, and some specific measures for self-employed and married women. The directives require member states to take action to implement these principles. Certain exceptions are allowed; for example, situations in which sex is a genuine occupational qualification.

In addition to its well-known action, and the consequences of it, about equal pay for work of equal value, the court has had considerable impact on British law and practice in matters relating to pensions and retirement. Examples of its rulings include an insistence that additional gross salary, forming employers' contributions to pension funds and benefits in kind payable after retirement, count as pay and must be equal; different state pensionable ages cannot justify employers compelling women and men to retire at different ages; if they have been compelled to retire earlier, women may claim compensation for loss of earnings; the benefits of company pension schemes must be equally accessible to men and women; part-timers must be included on a pro-rata basis; and the state allowance for the care of dependent relatives must be payable to married women as well as everyone else. Most of these rulings have reinforced campaigns to equalize the statutory pensionable age, currently exempt from Community regulation. One of the most popular possibilities has been that of flexibility for everyone between the ages of 60 and 65, though the Government favours the same age of 62 to 63 for all.

There are also 'permissive' Community measures which deal with the provision of services; for example, networks that monitor the availability of childcare and women's vocational (re)training. Funds for the latter may be available from the Social Fund and New Opportunities for Women programme. Though the European Parliament has criticized the paucity of the budget, it and the UK Women's Training Network have persuaded the commission that the cost of providing childcare for women trainees is a legitimate part of grant applications. The dissemination of information about such schemes depends on networking amongst progressive administrators and the voluntary sector within regions, across borders and between regions and Community institutions – a process that is both more observable in and obviously critical to the peripheries of the United Kingdom than at the level of central government.

Also in our workshop, Marie Stewart emphasized the need for equality policies to have an objective. It must be said that, while EC policies assist us to eliminate discrimination against individuals (and, in so doing sometimes have wider effects), they are not straightforward in their promotion of a goal of equal citizenship. As noted earlier, social rights are often thought of as integral to a modern concept of citizenship that involves ideas of agency and autonomy. Yet levels of material entitlements usually depend on employment. Men and women in the EC are still found in segregated occupations, associated with different levels of pay. The continuing domestic division of labour means that women are more likely than men to be employed seasonally and in part-time work. This means that the welfare entitlements of men and women are generally unequal. Policies which might have helped to reconcile work and family roles, such as those on positive action, part-time work and parental leave, have been vetoed or diluted – largely at the instigation of the UK government.

New, 'flexible' forms of employment are arising from the decline of traditional manufacturing, innovations in technology and the growth of the service sector, which could be managed so as to be advantageous to women. Though the Social Charter proposed some protection for 'atypical' work, the concept of 'worker' that underpins the EC concept of 'citizen' embodies the old conventions of full-time male employment. As a result, it is sometimes suggested that sex differences in society be acknowledged openly by giving women insurance credits for unpaid caring work. It is also acknowledged that this would institutionalize sexism, as it would not encourage flexibility in the distribution of social responsibilities. The advocates of this policy, however, see little sign of it coming about. It is equally unlikely that matters of culture, sexuality and violence, identified by a participant in the workshop as spheres of unequal legal protection, or perhaps the source of unequal citizenship, will become part of Community regulation – despite concerns about them expressed in the European Parliament.

Among those who appear to share an emphasis on the different social experience and/or sexuality of men and women, there is often a profound disagreement about whether differences are socially constructed or essential. This leads to a debate which tends to insist that men and women must be regarded as either the same or different and that their legal treatment must also be one or the other. In my view, these are false dichotomies; equal citizenship implies recognition of both similarities and differences, legal treatment being the same or different as appropriate. To be a citizen instead of a subject is to be able to define one's own needs and to influence the ways in which they are met. To be a citizen is to be able to take part in constructing a moral order that meets, or tries to meet, the legitimate needs of all.

Politics is always a contest over meanings. When the prime minister spoke of his 'victory' at Maastricht, he referred journalists to employers for objective confirmation that he had 'saved British jobs'. How could he think that this would clinch the argument? Employers have often used what seem to others to be irrational arguments and dubious facts when responding to women's claims for equality – for example, in connection with equalizing retirement ages. It is normal for contestants over policy formation to use definitions that are consistent with their outlooks. Employers, then, are no different except that, being more powerful, their definitions may be seen as more authoritative.

There are a number of examples of the positive impact of a culture of rights on the capacity of vulnerable citizens to succeed in having their meanings inscribed in public policy. In the United States, black men and women as well as women of different origins have been able to reconstruct traditional 'male' definitions of work and worker in the Fair Labor Standards Act, so as to achieve protection for farm workers and domestic servants – helped in their struggle by the idea that they were citizens entitled to claim common standards. Similarly, bodies of law in Scandinavia, enshrining what a good society aspires to, contribute to the confidence that women are full citizens. The American claimant's sense of political efficacy is replicated on the face of British women appearing on television after claiming rights in the European Court of Justice.

Objections to constitutional reform in this country often rest on the outlook of our judges. But, as Lord Scarman has pointed out, the absence of a guiding framework leaves them with nothing to fall back on when interpretations are necessary but their own sense of what is appropriate. At least in some areas of women's legal rights, existing EC provisions have given them something to go on. Despite Maastricht and defective formal channels of accountability in the Community, there are avenues through which national and trans-European groups of women can influence definitions of paid work, care and carers. Thus, women can shape at least a partial framework that recognizes their contributions to society and their rights as citizens. A democratic, pluralist constitution for the United Kingdom would surely fulfil a similar role.

9 'Race', Ethnicity and Constitutional Rights

Yasmin Ali

Up to now, questions of 'race' and citizenship have seemed sadly peripheral to the constitutional reform agenda. Yet any meaningful debate about democracy in Britain needs to encompass the experience of insecure minorities. Majority rights can never be secure as long as those of minorities are not respected. But more than that, the experience of minority ethnic communities in Britain reveals much about the failure of Britain to sustain and strengthen its democratic culture for all its citizens.

African-Caribbean and South Asian communities in Britain are often constructed as in some way fundamentally different from white communities and thus a 'problem'. The preferred solution to the 'problem' has been, from the earliest days of New Commonwealth settlement, to establish separate and parallel forms of mediation between minorities and the local state and other agencies. (Central government, significantly, has given local government the major responsibility for dealing with black communities, despite the trend towards centralization in other areas.) Rather than seek to renew local political cultures so that new communities could be integrated into democratic and accountable political channels (a process of renewal that might also have spared us the 'white riots' of the early 1990s), quasi-colonial structures were established whereby unelected community leaders were co-opted by local government, social services departments, the police and others to 'represent' their communities. Usually male, these leaders (and those to whom they reported) found it convenient to characterize communities as homogeneous, static and wholly consensual.

Although most minority ethnic communities have largely consisted of individuals who have the right to vote in Britain, and who often come from backgrounds of political activism in their countries of origin (see the early establishment in Britain of groups like the Indian Workers' Association, for example), it is through these parallel consultative mechanisms that they have learned to participate in British politics. At the heart of this system is patronage, as exercised by the local state in particular, but also by political parties.

In the absence of real political rights, there is some evidence of a growing reluctance among African-Caribbeans to get onto the electoral register, with a correspondingly very low level of turnout in elections, especially among young men. Yet far from being apathetic, research suggests that the level of interest in and awareness of political issues is actually higher amongst, young African-Caribbeans than it is amongst comparable white youths.[1] If there is alienation from the British political system, then it is in some ways a politically conscious and deliberate act of abstention. We need to ask how and why this situation has come about. The answers, I suspect, will reveal something not only about the way racism impacts upon the lives of young black people, but also about the nihilism among young white working-class men which is now coming to political attention. When people feel that they are victims of politics, that politics is something that is 'done to them', rather than feeling they are fellow participants in a democracy, something is badly wrong.

Asians vote in elections at much the same levels as white voters, and on the whole the issues which motivate all minority ethnic voters are the same as those which have salience to whites (the economy, health, education, etc.). Yet despite this, Asians have tended to be recruited into active politics, mainly through the Labour Party, as political ciphers serving the interests of small leadership groups. Manoeuvring political blocks and coalition building have taken precedence over political education. Discussion of political issues and their resolution by open democratic decision making are not an integral part of the experience of Labour Party membership, even for those who attend meetings. Instead, community leaders and local Labour leaders traded favours in return for delivering either patronage or votes. Encouraging a broader base of informed participation and accountable leadership has rarely been on the agenda for any of the main political parties, although there are some honourable exceptions which point the way towards a viable alternative politics.

The consequences are clear to see. For the Labour Party in particular, the failure to develop democratic practices which could encourage much wider participation in the party has resulted in some disastrous situations, such as those in Brent or Bradford where black political entrepreneurs, elevated to positions of greater individual power as councillors, have switched allegiance when a better 'deal' was offered by the Conservative Party. Former Bradford Labour councillor Mohammed Riaz, now a Conservative prospective parliamentary candidate, is perhaps the prime example of this process, although Brent's Conservative–Pan-Africanist coalition is more entertaining! Such acts have tended to reveal the limits of community leadership claims to be able to 'deliver' the votes of the community. Political entrepreneurs can use their access to party patronage to enhance their prestige just as long as there is some congruence between their ambitions and the political loyalties of the communities they claim to represent. When the limits are breached, black voters have tended to stick with party rather than individual loyalty, often with another individual coming along to fill the place of the departed leader. In such circumstances, 'ethnic' or religious loyalty has also failed to make much headway against basic political allegiances, as the poor showing of Islamic Party candidates in local elections has demonstrated.

When communities, and the often diverse interests within them, are misrepresented for the convenience of councils and the ambition of 'leaders', political tensions which ought to find expression through effective and legitimate political activity become distorted and squeeze out in surprising and sometimes destructive ways. Feelings of political exclusion and hopelessness engender damaging passivity punctuated by urban unrest. Much Muslim anger, and the forms it has taken over education and, particularly, *The Satanic Verses*, I believe to have material causes which might have been resolved or at least channelled constructively had British politics been more openly democratic and inclusive in character. The same can be said in some ways of all politically marginal communities, black and white.

There is an answer to the problem. It does not reside in reacting to the outward symptoms of minority disaffection, however, particularly not when it comes to a written constitution or a bill of rights. Ethnicity, even in the brief thirty-year history of most minority ethnic communities in Britain, has never been a stable and consensual basis for political identity and mobilization. Sometimes, as in the 1970s, nationalism and war have provided the basis for group identity, and indeed the politics of the homeland can still mobilize minorities in Britain, from the Irish to the supporters of a khalistani state. In many communities, smaller, older or more basic divisions define community identity, including caste, language or dialect, religious sectarianism and, increasingly, social class. The political impact of Islam, particularly as measured by media coverage of the Muslim Institute's Muslim Parliament, is another case in point, albeit one usually misunderstood. The overtly transnational, transracial and transethnic rhetoric of militant Islam is in practice regarded with deep suspicion and some resistance by many South Asian Muslims, whose cultural traditions and experience tend towards comfortable insularity rather than a politicized global perspective. Many a man who has argued approvingly for the *fatwa* would be appalled if his daughter wanted to marry a Muslim from the 'wrong' ethnic group, for example.

Most white people in Britain are never faced with the need to identify their own 'ethnic' identity, and they would inevitably have great difficulty if they tried, especially as a definition has to command group assent, not just individual preference. The question of ethnicity remains just as problematic for those of us who are compelled to characterize ourselves ethnically. Even those communities which have a high degree of consensus about who they are are increasingly being wrenched by the inevitable divisions within any community, particularly the dynamic of class and the changing expectations of women. In such circumstances, where identities are still being changed and contested, indeed where a new multiracial British identity is being developed, to write 'ethnic rights' into a constitution would be to entrench further the errors of multiculturalism which have so stoked the fires of communalism and introspection.

Racism, however, does need to be recognized. Individuals and communities do need the right not to be discriminated against, and that right should be fundamental. There is plentiful evidence of the enduring power of racism in employment, housing, education, the legal system and many other areas of life, despite nearly thirty years of anti-discrimination legislation; but equally there is evidence that where discrimination, overt or subtle, is ruled unacceptable, change can begin to occur. Indeed, the gradual acceptance of minority ethnic politicians in their own right by all political parties, from Paul Boateng on the Labour Treasury team to Baroness Flather, by way of Paddy Ashdown's effective community relations adviser Zerbanoo Gifford, all illustrate this process of change. But as yet progress is all too reversible. The absurd current situation whereby the Education Reform Act's 'right' of parental choice over the ethnic make-up of their child's school takes precedence over the Race Relations Act illustrates the weakness of anti-discrimination policy in Britain. The absence of interest in the European Community in acting against racial discrimination (in the context of a growth in electoral and 'street-level' support for the racist far right) further underlines the need for action.

There is a further point to be made about education, particularly as it is one of the most important political issues for minority ethnic communities. It is plainly unfair that Christian schools, governed in part by Christian clergy and showing preference to Christian pupils and teachers, are supported by public funds, whilst separate Muslim schools are not. It is, furthermore, such a glaring unfairness that it galvanizes support for Muslim schools, even from those who would not themselves have sought to use such facilities. The right to freedom of worship and entitlement to paid leave to celebrate major religious festivals are important, and must be underpinned by a guarantee of secular state education. A divided education system, especially one divided on religious lines (and effectively on racial lines) cannot be compatible with the development of a culture of democracy and inclusion.

For, above all, ethnic communities need to be included in, and involved in discussions about, a democratic renewal in Britain. Constitutional reform cannot be colour-blind whilst the evidence of structural inequality remains so apparent, but nor can it endorse ethnic absolutism for black communities whilst recognizing the dynamic and changing nature of white communities. Striking the right balance is a question of continual discussion and debate; but the discussion must take place at the centre, not on the periphery.

Critics of constitutional reform from both left and right often dismiss the matter by arguing that it is a middle-class obsession of no relevance to unemployed shipyard workers or East End Bangladeshis. They are wrong. By examining the rusting mechanisms of British democracy we begin to see what must link North Tyneside and Tower Hamlets, just as much as Hampstead and Headlingley. Britain needs a written constitution and an inclusively democratic political culture. But for us all to be citizens, we must recognize our right to be citizens in diverse ways. Oddly, that is the only way in which we can begin to recognize our similarities and strengthen our allegiances to one another.

Notes

1   See, for example, M. Fitzgerald, *Political Parties and Black People: Participation, Representation and Exploitation* (Runnymede Trust, London, 1984); Z. Layton-Henry and P.R. Rich (eds), *Race, Government and Politics in Britain* (Macmillan, Basingstoke, 1986); D. Studlar, *Non-White Policy Preferences, Political Participation and the Political Agenda in Britain*, in Layton-Henry and Rich, *Race, Government and Politics in Britain*.

Other useful books include:

G. Ben-Tovim et al., *The Local Politics of Race* (Macmillan, London, 1986).

W. Ball and John Solomos, *Race and Local Politics* (Macmillan, Hong Kong, 1990).

A.M. Messina, *Race and Party Competition in Britain* (Clarendon Press, Oxford, 1989).

H. Goulbourne (ed.), *Black Politics in Britain* (Gower, Aldershot, 1990).

Part III

Electoral Reform –
The Three Options

10   The Alternative Vote

Peter Hain MP

The current first-past-the-post system is unfair and the case for electoral reform is strong. But the fatal defect of all the major proportional representation (PR) systems is that the scope for local accountability is undermined, and power is sucked upwards to regional or national levels of the party structure.

The single transferable vote system, with on average five MPs in each 'multi-member' seat, would mean monster constituencies (some covering hundreds of square miles), so breaking the historic link between the local electorate and the MP. List systems would favour candidates approved by the party machine and local parties would lose virtually all influence. The additional member system favoured by most PR advocates in the Labour Party would mean two classes of MP: some constituency-based, the others constitutional free-loaders chosen from lists and without any constituency responsibilities. Furthermore, each PR option has almost as many idiosyncrasies as the current system, without its virtue of simplicity.[1]

Under PR, the ordinary voter would also have less opportunity to determine the composition of the government, because coalitions would become the norm rather than the exception. This was acknowledged by the political scientist Giovanni Sartori,[2] a proponent of an 'elitist' system of democracy. He argued quite unashamedly that PR would be a good thing because it invariably produces coalition governments, which make it difficult for the electorate to 'pin down who is responsible for decisions'! Another political scientist argued in similar terms that it would 'help protect the Parliamentary Labour Party from extra-parliamentary control'.[3] Small centre parties usually hold the balance of power under PR, exercising an influence quite out of proportion to their popular support, as for example in Germany and Israel.

A better option is the alternative vote (AV). Labour supported the AV in the period around and after World War I and carried it through the House of Commons in 1931, before it fell in the Lords. It is used in the Australian House of Representatives and retains single-member constituencies like the present ones. Rather than placing a mark against a single name, each voter numbers the candidates listed on the ballot paper in order of preference (for example, '1st: Green; 2nd: Democrat; 3rd: Labour'). If any candidate achieves an overall majority right away (that is, more than half the first preferences of voters on the first count), then he or she is elected. If not, the candidate with the lowest number of first votes, is eliminated, and second preferences of voters for him or her are allocated to the other candidates as indicated. This process is repeated through later counts, with bottom candidates falling out at each stage and their votes being allocated to those remaining, until one of these achieves an overall majority.

The main advantage of the AV over the existing system is that it requires winning candidates to secure a majority of votes, and this is a major, if not complete, step towards meeting the criticisms made by PR supporters. Crucially, by maintaining single-member seats it also maintains local accountability. However, although it secures a fairer relationship between seats and votes, the AV is strongly opposed by supporters of PR, mainly because it does not achieve genuine proportionality. Analysis of its impact by a London School of Economics study suggests gains for Labour and the Liberals at the expense of the Tories, who benefit disproportionately from the current system. The study assumed opinion polls showing the two major parties roughly level on about 40 per cent of the vote each.

The case for the AV is thus that:

It is fairer than first-past-the-post.

There is less scope for 'wasted' votes because electors could state their real first preference.

There would be less geographical bias of the kind which now sees the Tories overrepresented in the south.

Each MP would have to secure at least 50 per cent of the vote.

It is easier to form majority governments than under PR.

The single-member seat would be retained.

It is relatively simple, a virtue not without merit and which contrasts with the almost unfathomable complexities of most PR options.

It does not require boundary changes, making it much easier and quicker to implement.

By-elections would be easy to organize.

It is also the only option the Commons would probably back, since MPs are hardly likely to vote themselves out of their own seats, and this highly practical matter should not be underestimated if the intention to reform is serious; one need only examine the debates and behaviour of MPs when the issue was last a major one in the post-World War I period to find confirmation.

However, if the AV is adopted it should be in parallel to the replacement of the House of Lords by a democratic second chamber elected under a list system of PR. This would enable the aspirations for completely proportional representation to be met in at least one half of Parliament, whilst also producing a second chamber that could genuinely claim legitimacy as a constitutional check by containing a fair spread of almost all political opinion from the Greens upwards. It could be elected from party lists according to the regional vote their party polled in the same general election. The same vote given to a parliamentary candidate locally would be allocated to that candidate's party in a regional pool. The percentage of that pool received by each party would determine their allocation of second chamber members from the region concerned. The objection to the list principle argued above does not apply in this case, since members of the second chamber do not have any constituent duties or representative responsibilities.

This would also allow positive action to secure a fair representation of women, the regions and ethnic minorities. For example, the Labour Party could select its regional lists for the second chamber by democratic vote of either regional members or conferences, and we could build in quotas, thus satisfying legitimate claims for fair representation within the party in a way that cannot be enforced whilst retaining local autonomy in selections.

By such an approach, we could combine the advantages of the single-member seat and the prospect of being able to form a single-party government, with a reform of the second chamber which satisfied the demand for fairer representation. This could form the basis for a new agenda for electoral reform that is both more credible and practical than those offered by other groups supporting the principle.

Notes

1 For a detailed analysis and evidence see my *Proportional Misrepresentation* (Wildwood House, London, 1986).
2 G. Sartori, *Democratic Theory* (Frederick Praeger, New York, 1965), p. 107.
3 H. Berrington, 'Electoral reform and national government', in S.E. Finer (ed.), *Adversary Politics and Electoral Reform* (Anthony Wigram, London, 1975), p. 288.

11 The Single Transferable Vote

Michael Meadowcroft

The failure of the opposition parties to capitalize on the electoral reform issue in the 1992 general election campaign in the face of John Major's outright opposition to proportional representation (PR) demonstrated the febrility of the reformers' case. The anti-PR case is a minority position but, with the pro case split, in varying degrees, between Labour, Liberal Democrat and the Nationalist parties, it was cleverly used to the electoral advantage of the Conservative Party.

Rather than benefiting the Labour and Liberal Democrat parties as they imagined it would, the emphasis on constitutional issues, including electoral reform, over the last ten days of the election campaign turned out to be a liability, albeit a minor one. All Labour could say was that the party was examining the need for electoral reform and had an open mind. Votes were simply not going to fall into the lap of any party that simply made vaguely sympathetic noises about 'PR'. Labour's tentativeness exposed its inability to combat the knee-jerk slogans ritually trotted out against proportional representation. For their part, the Liberal Democrats, despite their official policy in favour of the single transferable vote (STV), also suffered from vacillation on their preferred system, with Paddy Ashdown's office briefing the press that the party would accept *any* proportional system on offer. Furthermore, the Liberal Democrats never escaped the charge of wanting PR from selfish motives – even though retention of the present system by the Conservatives lays them wide open to precisely the same charge.

The lessons from the 1992 election are clear. To transform the electoral reform question from an issue which is right and just into one which is also a vote-winner requires an intellectual understanding of the principles that underpin electoral reform, plus a firm commitment to the electoral system that best meets national and international political needs. The different voting systems on offer produce fundamentally different political cultures, and unless there is a meeting of minds on what kind of *politics* the electoral reform supporters want there is unlikely to be agreement on a preferred system, and opponents will once again have a field day. The urgent task, therefore, is to move the argument from *whether* to change on to *what* change to make. With agreement on a preferred system, it may just be possible to envisage cooperation between opposition parties in order to ensure the crucial change. Without agreement, the Conservatives may well be able to manipulate the present system yet again.

There is no perfect voting system, not least because some of the criteria one seeks from a system are to some extent in conflict. For instance, an emphasis on party proportionality means party lists and thus cuts across the desire for the accountability of individual elected representatives to their electors. A concern for equal value of votes tends to require the existence of more rather than fewer parties, and thus can be inimical to the criterion of effective choice between potential governments. Despite the tensions between them, these four criteria are fundamental to every discussion of electoral reform. There are others, of course: a desire for 'strong government', for instance, if perceived as providing an artificially exaggerated majority in Parliament, runs counter to the need for consent: but the four emphasized above are a valuable yardstick against which to measure the different systems. I believe that the intra- and inter-party debate, and public discussion, between now and the next election should focus on determining which electoral system best meets these criteria.

Listing the Dangers

I assume that the case against first-past-the-post is accepted in principle and that the system's defects are well recognized. It fails to produce a representative Parliament; it brings about a country dangerously divided on national and regional lines; it diminishes the enfranchisement of over half the electorate; it encourages negative voting against the most disliked party or candidate, and therefore discourages positive and rigorous debate; it reduces the possibility of the voters securing sympathetic help from their members; and, by requiring in effect a party list of one, it gives immense power to the party which, by its selection of the candidate, effectively chooses the MP in a majority of seats.[1] The question here is, therefore, which should be the alternative around which all those in favour of reform should unite.

All systems that involve party lists are dangerous. To one degree or another, they all give too much power to the individual party. By requiring the elector to vote for a party rather than a candidate, they necessitate the party drawing up a list of its candidates, almost invariably in priority order, so that which individual candidates are elected depends on the percentage vote gained by the party and where the cut-off point thus comes down the list. The individual candidate has virtually no external direct influence with the electors on his or her election, but always has to work internally to retain the party's approval. Party lists breed conformity and deter individuality. At a time when the insidious growth of hegemonic party politics, and the consequent diminution of pluralism, is threatening democracy at both national and local levels, the last thing we need is an electoral system which enables this lethal trend to continue.

The worst effects of list systems are sometimes mitigated by allowing the voter to vote to vary the order set out by the party. This is certainly an improvement, but experience suggests that there is still a significant predisposition to accept the party's order and, because this easy option is available, it encourages neither deeper involvement nor greater sophistication. Also, in virtually every example, unlike STV, it only allows the voter to express individual preferences between candidates of one party. The dangers of the list system are vividly seen in Central and Eastern Europe. A requirement to vote for a single list emphasizes separateness, encourages parties based on regional and ethnic identities rather than on political philosophy, and tends inexorably to atomization and instability. STV, on the other hand, by its nature, encourages party linkages and an emphasis on cross-party similarities, particularly on broad philosophy. As such it maximizes and encourages unity and integration. This is particularly crucial in the context of current international conflict and disarray.

List systems require either an acceptance that, in the United Kingdom, any party securing a 651st share of the national vote is entitled to one seat, with an inevitable proliferation of small parties in Parliament, or the imposition of an artificial threshold – 5 per cent in Germany – below which a party is denied any representation. Neither alternative is particularly satisfactory. The former has led to the caricaturing of Israel and Italy by opponents of PR, who can point out the apparent inability of their politicians to form governments or to resolve their entrenched political problems. The latter has led to an almost permanent single pivotal party, the Free Democrats, whose decision whether to ally with the Social Democrats or Christian Democrats determines who shall govern Germany – in one case they even changed partners in mid-parliament.

The German system has, of course, the further sophistication of the double ballot whereby, on the same ballot paper, the voter votes first for a constituency MP and secondly for a party preference. Superficially this appears attractive, but it is seriously flawed.[2] It only survives in Germany because there is no tradition there of members of the Bundestag undertaking constituency casework – this is regarded as a very important responsibility by most British MPs. In Germany there is no intrinsic difference in the perception of the role of members elected from constituencies or from the list. The position in Britain would be very different: MPs would have constituencies twice the present size, half the MPs would have to endeavour to represent these huge elec-torates, trying to cope with twice the present caseload, while the other half, elected from the list, could either swan around or – even more infuriating – quite legitimately 'interfere' in any constituency they chose to target for political reasons. Rather than preserving the con-stituency link, this is likely to undermine it.

Under this additional member system (AMS), the constituency half of the ballot plays no part in influencing which party or parties can form a government, as the parties' seat totals in the Bundestag are deter-mined by the percentages polled on the list ballot. With it also comes the inevitable spectacle of MPs defeated in a constituency being elected from the list; indeed, it is not unknown for all three candidates from a constituency to be elected. AMS would not be supported for an instant by any party if candidates were only permitted to stand in one of the two ballots.

Some supporters of AMS, recognizing that the British electorate, with its tradition of voting for candidates rather than parties, is unlikely to be particularly keen to use the double ballot, have proposed that the voter's choice of candidate should be assumed also to be that elector's choice of party, and that the number of additional members for each party should be calculated by extrapolating these personal votes. This suggestion effectively removes the right of an elector to vote differently on the two ballots, both in order to support the best-placed constituency candidate and also for their preferred party on the list – which is about the only point in AMS's favour. It has also been suggested that to avoid the parties determining the order of their lists, a system of awarding seats to a party's 'best losers' should be devised. Quite apart from the dubious principle of rejected candidates being slipped in, Vernon Bogdanor has pointed out that this would be worse than a lottery, depending on the marginality of seats and the number of parties contesting them.[3] AMS is the worst of all worlds, combining the defects of first-past-the-post with the dangers of the party list.

Preferential Benefits

The best electoral system is already being used in public elections in the United Kingdom. The single transferable vote was introduced for the Northern Ireland Assembly elections of 1973, and for all local elections there, by the Conservative government of the day, with Opposition support. The government also produced an excellent pamphlet, *It's as Easy as 1, 2, 3 . . .* , to show how simple and straightforward STV is. A Labour government confirmed STV as the system to be used in Northern Ireland for the European Parliament election of 1979 and thereafter. In the first election for the Assembly under STV, in 1973, every constituency returned at least one representative from each side of the community. There was a 70 per cent turnout and only 2.3 per cent spoiled papers. Even at the European elections, with a single constituency for the whole of Northern Ireland, the count took only slightly longer than many first-past-the-post counts.

For the voter, STV is simple. Every constituency elects a number of MPs – in the Republic of Ireland, between three and five. Each elector is asked to put into an order of preference as many of the candidates as he or she has an opinion on. Thus the elector numbers the candidates 1, 2, 3 and so on. The ballot paper therefore indicates the voter's individual and specific instructions to the Returning Officer at the count: 'I have indicated the candidate I most want to represent me; if that candidate has so many votes that mine is not needed for his or her election, then please take my second choice into consideration, and so on down my list. On the other hand, if my first choice has no chance of being elected then please go on to my next choice.' So long as the voter is content that the counting process is fair – and the presence at the count of representatives of all parties guarantees that it is – then he or she need not worry about the mathematics of the counting process.

The principle behind the count is straightforward. The minimum figure that guarantees election is determined. This is the quota for election and is the total number of votes cast divided by one more than the number of seats available, plus one vote. Any candidate with more first preferences than this quota is deemed elected, and his or her surplus votes above the quota are distributed to the indicated second-preference candidates. Because only parts of the voters' first preferences were needed to elect a candidate, the unused parts of those votes are transferred to their second preferences at an appropriate reduced value; that is, the votes above the quota divided by the total first preferences. Thus if a candidate has 200 first preferences and the quota is 100, the surplus votes are distributed at 0.5 each, because the candidate only needed half of each vote to be elected. If at any stage no candidate has enough first preferences to be elected, then the bottom candidate is excluded and that candidate's votes are distributed according to the second preferences. Because the first preferences did not elect a candidate, the distribution is at their full value. Transferring surpluses and excluding bottom candidates continues until all the seats are filled.

Unlike all single-member electoral systems, STV gives proportionality – if voters wish to vote only for their party's candidates, the candidates will be duly elected in proportion to those votes. It provides a natural threshold – in a five-member seat, a party must get one-sixth of the vote to guarantee winning one seat. It preserves the constituency link and gives better accountability than the present system – the team of MPs in a constituency is likely to include someone from almost every elector's preferences. It enhances political debate and encourages a more thoughtful attitude towards politics – it is impossible simply to vote negatively in a preferential voting system, and it removes the 'safe-seat' syndrome that enables candidates and parties to avoid public debate. It gives effective choice and encourages 'natural' coalitions – voters' preferences indicate the party links they prefer. It provides a healthy balance between individual candidates and their parties – popular individuals will run ahead of their parties under STV, as the voter can choose within and across parties. It encourages more women and ethnic minority candidates – to maximize their vote in a multi-member constituency, parties are likely to put up a balanced team of candidates.

And it minimizes 'wasted' votes – virtually every elector gets a representative to whom he or she gave a high preference on the ballot paper.

Conclusion

Existing MPs ought to go for STV: sitting members with a good track record are very likely to be at an advantage under a preferential system. It works well in both parts of Ireland and the legislation exists for easy implementation. Above all, it empowers the voter in a unique way. No other system satisfies the four criteria of proportionality, accountability, equal value and effective choice to anywhere near the same degree. STV is the best system for demolishing the tired old anti-PR jibes of adherents to the present system. It offers the best opportunity for uniting the case for electoral reform, and is therefore the most effective.

References

1 For a more detailed consideration of the myths surrounding single-member seats, see Michael Meadowcroft, *The Politics of Electoral Reform* (Electoral Reform Society, London, 1991).
2 For a fuller analysis of the additional member system, see Vernon Bogdanor, *Electoral Reform – Which System?* (Electoral Reform Society, London, 1992).
3 Ibid.
4 Northern Ireland Office, *It's as Easy as 1, 2, 3 . . .* (The Northern Ireland Office, 1972).

12 *Vorsprung Durch* AMS

Austin Mitchell MP

I am not Paddy Ashdown, so I will not argue that the electoral system I prefer will transform humanity and regenerate politics and the economy. There is, in fact, no perfect electoral system. I would make only two simple claims of any. First, it must bring politics and society into harmony, something ours no longer does. British politics cannot make the transition to pluralism which a changed social base now requires. In that situation the electoral system throws up bizarre results – like Margaret Thatcher's dictatorship of the minority. Second, the system must be fair. That means proportionality. Mass democracy is party democracy; parties must be represented in proportion to the votes cast for them. Otherwise people have no identification with Parliament or the government.

My politics are those of liberty, equality and fraternity. So I want a system which is democratic, gives every vote a more or less equal value, and brings the community together by giving everyone a stake in the result. You cannot build fair, democratic structures on an unfair electoral system, and the longer we continue to try, the more messy our politics will become.

We must, therefore, abolish first-past-the-post. It may have worked well when there were two blocks of permanent, committed supporters, and the electoral system had to take the small shifts among 'floating voters' and amplify them into a bigger change in seats to produce a strong government, which accurately represented – most times but not always – what the people wanted. Since then, however, the blocks have shrunk, more people are open to change, more choose other parties, and more want influence over government, not just a vote every four years which does not achieve much. Society has become more volatile: the electoral system itself has become more rigid. The number of marginal seats is half what it was, as the south becomes more Conservative, the north more Labour.

So we must free up the system and give the people more power over the parties. Only PR (proportional representation) can do that. Reject, with first-past-the-post, the alternative vote, a soft option which some might support but which does nothing to give Labour voters in the south a return on their vote or to make the system proportional. It might help the Liberals, as everyone's second preference. Yet it also leads to people casting a negative rather than a positive vote. That could keep us out of power, as it did Labour in Australia for two decades.

So PR, but which system? Systems exclusively based on lists give the parties too much power. We already have too many conformist clones to want that. The single transferable vote (STV) is not proportional enough. It works in Ireland because they have not got a developed party system like ours, merely historical accidents preserved in the STV deep freeze. STV makes parties and politics obsessively local, drags everything down to the local pork barrel, and focuses MPs exclusively on constituencies when they compete against each other and against those in local government who seek to displace them. Under it, we would all beat the local drum.

Which leaves us with the additional member system (AMS). First, the respectable 'official arguments' for it: it works well in Germany, and most serious inquiries into electoral systems have endorsed it, as the Royal Commission did in New Zealand and the Hansard Society inquiry did here. The practical arguments are that it keeps constituencies, which any MP who is as proud of his constituency as I am must want. Yet it also gives the parties a role, through regional lists. This is the best of both worlds and recognizes that there are two types of MP: devoted constituency workers and 'ministrables' – people of destiny, above such mundane matters.

AMS makes coalitions more likely. Any PR system will. Yet it does give electors influence on the coalition process, for they have two votes, which can be cast in different ways and often are. Parties usually make their preferred coalition partners clear before the campaign, so the use of the second vote allows electors to react to that.

Because the system is very flexible, it can be modified to suit our purposes. We can vary the size of the threshold against fascists and lunatics; We can have local or national thresholds. The proportion of additional members added to top up the constituency section can be varied. We can determine the nature of selections for the list by party, primary election or other means. We can even adopt it to facilitate a gradual transition from our present system to PR by increasing the top-up element, though I have to say that I would prefer change at one fell swoop.

We gave AMS to Germany after the war. Let us take it back and enjoy it. With a very similar party and social system, we could benefit in the same way. Germany has developed a democracy which, for all our condescending disapproval of the master race, works better, is far more serious and far healthier than our own. All the citizen's charters in the world will not do as much to set the people free and give them a real influence as AMS. We cannot get to that particular beach before the Germans, but we can have one of our own and be as democratic as they.

Part IV

Constitutional Reform and Economic Performance

13 Evicting the Rentier State

Will Hutton

The victor's spoils in a British election campaign are more complete than those in any other advanced democracy. To the winner fall untrammelled executive powers and near-complete discretion in how they are used – for the runner up, the lack of power is total.

Small wonder at the presidential nature of the competition; what is at stake is more power than most presidents have ever dreamed of exercising. All the sound and fury is to help gain control of a pre-modern set of institutions whose capacity to represent the notion of the commonweal is rapidly fading. There is instead a medieval construct, colonized by Conservatives, whose function has become the provision of administration rather than democratic government.

The root of the decay is the way royal prerogative power has combined with control of the House of Commons to allow complete dominance over the formulation of law, its passing into legislation and its subsequent adjudication. Instead of separating executive, legislative and judicial powers, Britain has organized them into a de facto union, thus according to the government of the day an unparalleled concentration of potential power. It is this that 13 years of Conservatism has exploited.

The casualties abound, from the emasculation of the idea of local government to the promotion of Conservative partisans to the highest level of the Civil Service. But the most dangerous consequence of the biases in Britain's state structures are that they are essential reinforcing elements in the pervasive culture of the rentier – the philosophy in which the ultimate object of life is to own a rent or any other stream of income and gain security. Because government passes into the ownership of the majority party, the reflex instinct of our governors is that of rentier landlords. They do not have to engage in a continuing relationship with those whose assets they are administering, nor have a dialogue with those whose view of the world differs from their own.

So it is that British budget making, for example, takes on its particular hue, with landlord chancellors dolling out favours or penalties to those who suit their ideological prejudices, and the results automatically becoming law. So it is that rentier Conservatism has not cared about the character of Britain's economic structure – service sector or manufacturing, domestic- or foreign-owned – as long as the taxes are paid and the people more or less employed. And as good rentiers, the emphasis is on keeping inflation down, more than anything else.

The consonance of the values of the state with those of the Conservative Party could not be more obvious. After all, it has been Conservatism that has been the principal beneficiary of Britain's state structures – at least until now. Margaret Thatcher's genius was to weld the values of the rentier – property rights, low taxes and minimal government – together with those of party and state, and at the same time convert enough of the electorate to the same values to win three elections. But rentierdom has proved the Conservative Party's downfall; financial deregulation, high exchange rates and interest rates, and the roll-back of the state have collapsed into deindustrialization, recession and widespread poverty.

For Labour, the problem is that it is competing for control of a rentier state while proclaiming the values of industry, participation and equality; if it is not to be converted into a social democratic rentier, then it must pay attention to the state structures and values it will inherit. This has happened before, with trade unions and local authorities looking to colonize the state via Labour support. For it to happen again would be unforgivable.

Nor are these minority concerns; an NOP poll for Charter 88, whose Democracy Day debates across the country were among the most significant events of the 1992 election campaign, reported that two-thirds of the electorate believes the system of government is not working properly. There is an appetite for more democratic integrity. And reform is not merely a matter of introducing a fair voting system, as the Liberal Democrats constantly stress, so that at least those who come to run the state would more accurately reflect public opinion. The majority coalition parties in the House of Commons would still be untrammelled masters of all they surveyed – and the landlord culture at the quick of British government would remain.

To lay the foundations of a truly democratic state requires a much more comprehensive approach. The hegemony of the south east and its preoccupations in government decision making needs to be challenged by empowering not only Scotland and Wales, but also the north of England. In this respect, Scottish proponents of independence have their strongest case: devolution of powers which leaves the rentier English state in place is valueless. Devolution only has meaning in the context of a wider constitutional settlement which allows the proper expression of public interest and all the dynamizing consequences that flow from it; only with such a settlement can the urge for Scottish independence be satisfied.

But participation in decision making is not possible without information – and information is still closely guarded by our landlord masters. Whether it is the government's possible collusion in selling arms to Iraq or the privatization of British Rail, it is no longer good enough to treat the public like children, with information doled out as the state decrees fit. Again, secrecy learnt in the public domain spills over to the private; access to information is indivisible and British business should be as open as the state. Perhaps, for example, if the public had known more about the loan structure of British banks, they might have made fewer mistakes with the money.

Information and devolution of power, however, are no use if the state retains discretionary power; which is why, as the fathers of democracy argued, the arms of the state should be formally separated. In Britain they are fused.

A legal system preoccupied with upholding the rentier state has meant that basic justice – from protection from overmighty creditors to appeal over wrongful imprisonment – is ever harder to obtain unless you are rich and prepared to wait. But again, reform in one area requires attention in another; a separate judiciary needs in turn a separation of the legislature and executive. The solution is to make the House of Lords an elected second chamber with the capacity to block laws like the poll tax for which there is no majority in the country. This does not mean there will never again be unwanted law, but it greatly reduces the risk.

These are all great prizes. They will transform the character of our parties, politics and economy – and rescue the notion of public interest from the slough into which it has sunk. On the chess board of the British political economy, the City of London, may be the queen, but the constitution is the king. Labour must not allow its relief that occasionally the system allows it a share of the spoils to obscure its mission. Rentier England will only be checkmated when Labour moves on the king.

14 Collaborative Capitalism and Constitutional Change

David Marquand

Few would dispute that the character of an economy depends in part on the character, conduct and culture of the state. Even those who believe that the competitive free market is bound, by definition, to allocate resources more efficiently than any other mechanism, and that public intervention in the economy does more harm than good, accept that governments can affect economic behaviour for good or ill – for good by removing barriers to free competition, and for ill by erecting or maintaining them. Other schools of thought hold that, at least in principle, state intervention can either improve economic performance, or at least facilitate its improvement.

Except in very broad terms, however, the nature of the connection is far from clear. Early nineteenth-century Britain, late nineteenth-century Germany and present-day Japan have all been economic success stories, but their political institutions differed sharply from each other. There is not much doubt that, over the long haul and in time of peace, capitalist market economies perform better than socialist command economies (though it is worth remembering that the forced industrialization of Stalin's Soviet Union created one of the most impressive war machines in the history of the world). But capitalist market economies come in a variety of forms, and so do the regimes that correspond to them. The widely held notion that there is a necessary connection between capitalism, the free market and democracy is an illusion. Pinochet's Chile had a capitalist free market, but it was not a democracy. The economy of Hitler's Germany was unmistakably capitalist, but only dubiously free market.

By the same token, it is impossible to establish a clear connection between economic performance and any particular set of constitutional arrangements. The constitution of the United States has altered very little in the last hundred years. A hundred years ago, the American economy was, by most indices, the most successful in the world. In the last thirty years or so, it has been one of the least successful. Gaullist France and pre-unification Federal Germany were both democracies, but their versions of democracy could scarcely have been more different. Both were hugely successful in economic terms. (Whether post-unification Germany will be equally successful remains to be seen.) Much the same applies in reverse. In the 1970s, it was widely believed that Britain's relative economic decline could be attributed to the sharp oscillations of policy produced by 'adversary politics'; and that electoral reform would produce the policy continuity needed to put things right.[1] The 1980s saw a long period of policy continuity, albeit in a still-adversarial system, but relative decline continued.

Yet it would be wrong to end the story there. The connections between the character and conduct of the state, the rules set out in its constitution, the understandings and codes of behaviour encapsulated in those rules and the performance of the economy are complex, subtle and poorly understood, but that does not mean that there is no connection. Constitutions, after all, define the terms on which public power is distributed and on which it can legitimately be exercised. Only on the heroic, and surely absurd, assumption that public power can have no influence whatever on economic performance could that definition be economically irrelevant. On a deeper, and perhaps more important, level, a constitution is a kind of distillation of a political community's view of its better self: an embodiment of its conception of the nature of politics, of the sources of political authority and ultimately of the good society: a mirror reflecting its public philosophy and most cherished values. And, in mirroring values, constitutions also reinforce them. They help to tell the members of a political community who they are and how they ought to behave. Since the members of a political community are also actors in an economy, the message has an economic dimension as well as a political one.

Looked at against that background, the debate over constitutional reform in contemporary Britain takes on a new significance. As everyone knows, the British constitution is uncodified, a jumble of sometimes ambiguous precedents, not a document which any citizen can obtain and read. But its message is no less insistent for that. At its core lies the ancient doctrine of the absolute sovereignty of the crown-in-

Parliament; and the values which that doctrine mirrors and reinforces are only too clear. They are hierarchical, not participatory; monist, not pluralist; in a profound sense, pre-democratic, not democratic. The vision of the good society which they encapsulate and underpin is one in which the rulers rule and the ruled know their place: in which legitimate power flows from the top down, not from the bottom up; in which public policy is the property of the rulers, not of the ruled; and in which decisions are made in the south-eastern core, not in the periphery. In our time, the powers of the absolutely sovereign crown-in-Parliament have, of course, been at the disposal of the victors in a democratic election. The democratic radicals of the nineteenth century did not win all their battles, but they did win some of them. Because their victory was incomplete, however, democracy came to this country as a thief in the night rather than as a conqueror at the gates. Our *ancien régime* withstood the great revolutions of eighteenth-century America and France, which served as the crucibles for the modern ideal of equal citizenship; it beat off the Napoleonic revolution on horseback; and it remained untouched by the upheavals of 1848. Though it expired in the end, it stamped its quasi-democratic successor with its impress. New men, new groups and, even the occasional new woman were admitted into the political establishment. But it changed them more than they changed it. It was still the same old establishment, its values and assumptions were still hierarchical, and the powers it exercised were still the crown's and not the people's.

It would be absurd to suggest that these values are directly responsible for Britain's relative economic decline, but there is growing evidence that they and the public philosophy with which they are associated stand in the way of the changes of culture and practice which are the prerequisites of economic success in our time. As the French economist, Michel Albert, has brilliantly argued,[2] there are at least two models of capitalism, not one. One is what he calls the 'neo-American' model, found in its most developed form in the United Kingdom and the United States, and based on individual success and short-term profit. The other is the 'Rhenish' model of Switzerland, Germany, the Low Countries, Scandinavia and, with some variations, Japan. Its central elements are consensus, collective success and concern for the long term. By almost any index, the 'Rhenish' model has been triumphantly successful; in our time, the 'neo-American' model has been a dismal failure. The question is, why?

Both are capitalist. In both, the means of production are largely in private hands; in both, resources are allocated largely through the market; both are dominated by private, profit-seeking firms which compete for custom and stand or fall by their ability to pass the tests of the market-place. In a struggle between capitalism and socialism, both are therefore on the same side. But it is only because that struggle has loomed so large for so long that we have failed to see that, in most other respects, the 'neo-American' and 'Rhenish' models are profoundly different, perhaps even antagonistic. 'Rhenish' capitalism is, of course, competitive. The yardstick of profitability has to be satisfied. But it is also collaborative. It depends on a subtle symbiosis of competition and cooperation, underpinned by corporatist or quasi-corporatist institutions and practices which the neo-classical economic doctrines of the Anglo-American tradition would condemn as protectionist and therefore inefficient. In short, its market is not the famous 'undistorted' market of the Anglo-American economics profession and the Anglo-American political class. What the Anglo-American tradition sees as distortions, impeding free competition, it sees as the necessary conditions of competitive success.

Success has been forthcoming – and on a scale which would have seemed inconceivable as recently as a generation ago. The reasons are complex. The notion of the 'social market', which British politicians often trot out as an explanation, merely confuses the issue. The 'social market', as understood in this country, is an Anglo-American-style free market, mitigated by a rather offensive kind of 'compassion'. But the point about 'Rhenish' capitalism is that the market does not operate on Anglo-American lines; that it is not driven by individual self-interest and the search for profit in the short term; that market forces are constrained by dense and complex networks of intersecting interests, held together by solidaristic values and cooperative habits.

Because of all this, market actors are able to take a long view – above all, in respect of human capital. The system as a whole trades off losses in the short-term efficiency on which the Anglo-American tradition focuses against gains in the public goods of consensual adaptation and social peace. It owes its extraordinary success to its capacity to make that trade-off. For, in a sophisticated economy, human capital holds the key to competitive power, with the result that consensual adaptation and social peace become ever more valuable. By the same token, the possessive, inevitably short-term, individualism that drives the neo-American model becomes self-stultifying. Against that background, the precipitate relative decline of the British economy over the last fifty years, and of the American over the last thirty, ceases to be a matter for surprise.

Unfortunately, however, 'Rhenish' capitalism is poorly understood – above all, of course, in English-speaking economic cultures, saturated with the presuppositions of mainstream Anglo-American economics. For it has no ideology. It is a practice, not a doctrine. It has grown up higgledy-piggledy, through trial and error, negotiation and compromise; and it has never been theorized. Its exponents have no texts, no sacred books, no simple cries. All they can do is to point to a complex and messy reality which takes time and hard work to understand. Its delicate symbiosis between competition and collaboration, the networks of intersecting interests and cooperative practices on which it depends, depend on tacit understandings and uncodified assumptions which are almost incomprehensible to those brought up in the Anglo-American tradition.

That does not mean, however, that there is nothing more to be said. In an important study, Jonathan Boswell argues that the key to the success of the 'Rhenish' model (not that he uses the term) lies in a notion of economic community 'fundamentally opposed' both to the liberal individualism which lies at the heart of mainstream Anglo-American economics, and to conventional collectivism.[3] An economic community would be:

> a complex of connecting cells whose mutual sensitivities represent a vital force. . . . The economic organisations themselves are to be associates or social partners . . .
> Neither intimacy nor a constant huddling together is envisaged, let alone unanimity. The social partners are to be strung together by elastic bands, not cords or chains. On the other hand, analogies from conventional political understandings, international relations or the sports field are too slack. Economic community involves a lot more than, say, common membership of a nation state, non-belligerent coexistence or joint involvement in a competitive game.
> The whole network is to be interwoven by mutual responsibilities. No 'invisible hand' is expected to harmonize the different parts. Mere balance or competition among the separate interests contributes little to, may often detract from, the common good. Nor is obedience to the state and the law to be loaded with the inordinate burden of producing that common good. Rather, public responsibilities as well as powers are to be widely diffused among economic agents.[4]

This is plainly a world away from individualistic economic liberalism and collectivist state socialism. Less obviously, it is equally far removed from the British version of the post-war mixed economy: from the system described by Andrew Shonfield, celebrated by Anthony Crosland and managed, with diminishing success, by the governments of the 1950s, 1960s and 1970s. For that system never got beyond belligerent coexistence. A jealous political class, imbued with the preconceptions of parliamentary absolutism, refused to diffuse public responsibilities and powers among economic agents, while an archaic economic culture, suffused with the assumptions of possessive individualism, failed to adapt to technological change. The great economic organizations never became social partners. There was no network of mutual responsibilities. Hence the Hobbesian *sauve qui peut* which overwhelmed the governments of the 1970s and which paved the way for the renaissance of individualistic economic liberalism in the 1980s.

Plainly, there is no simple short cut to a Boswellian economic community. No conceivable set of constitutional changes could, of themselves, transplant the 'Rhenish' model to British soil. As plainly, however, the values and practices transmitted and legitimized by the British doctrine of absolute parliamentary sovereignty are incompatible with it. As Boswell points out, the delicate symbiosis between competition and collaboration which he anatomizes depends on four crucial factors. There must be reasonable continuity in the membership and direction of the organizations whose cooperation is the prerequisite of a cooperative economy. They must not be so small or so numerous that they have no concern for the public interest or so big and so few that they dwarf the political authorities. Their activities must be sufficiently transparent to be monitored by those they affect, and – even more importantly – by the wider society. There must be forums in which they learn the norms of cooperation. Above all, the public philosophy of the society in which they act must give a high place to the values of fraternity, association and participation. Current British constitutional doctrine – and, still more, the values and presuppositions embedded in it – bars the way to all of these.

That, however, is only the beginning of the story. At the heart of Albert's 'Rhenish' capitalism and of Boswell's 'economic community' lies a conception of the individual, and of the proper relationship between the individual and the community, which is alien, not just to British constitutional doctrine, but to the entire British political tradition. Lockean liberalism is no more congruent with it than is Hobbesian absolutism; Fabian social democrats are as remote from it as is the Hayekian new right and the Bennite new left. But most British constitutional reformers are, at heart, Lockean liberals. They base their case against Westminster absolutism, implicitly or explicitly, on a demand for, and an assertion of, individual rights; behind that demand lies the assumption that, in some profound sense, the individual is prior to the community. The notions that rights imply duties, that individuals are shaped by a community which is more than the sum of its parts, and realize themselves fully only by discharging their obligations to it, make them uneasy. Yet notions of this sort are part of the soil in which 'Rhenish' capitalism has grown. A Lockean constitution, based on the notion of citizenship rights, would, in practice, devolve power, encourage transparency and facilitate pluralism. As such, it would be a great advance on the Hobbesian constitution we now know. But it would not, in itself, procure the changes of culture and assumption which a transition to collaborative capitalism would make necessary. In this perspective, at any rate, constitutional reform is not a solution but a catalyst, not a destination but a starting point.

Notes

1   See, in particular, S.E. Finer (ed.), *Adversary Politics and Electoral Reform* (Wigram, London, 1975). For a powerful critique, see A.M. Gamble and S.A. Walkland, *The British Party System and Economic Policy 1945–1983:Studies in Adversary Politics* (Clarendon Press, Oxford, 1984).

2   Michel Albert, *Capitalisme Contre Capitalisme* (Editions du Seuil, Paris, 1991).

3   Jonathan Boswell, *Community and the Economy: The Theory of Public Co-operation* (Routledge, London, 1990), p. 54.

4   Ibid., p. 54.

15 The Constitution of the Economy in an Age of Human Capital

Geoff Mulgan

Introduction

When a large firm in Britain or the United States is taken over, often after a vicious battle to secure the support of a handful of major institutional shareholders, its constitutional position is cast into stark relief. What looks at first glance like a hypermodern global institution, at ease in the age of the satellite and the automated factory, is revealed as archaic and unreformed: left behind in the nineteenth-century model of the joint-stock, limited-liability company that predates even majority suffrage. Financial capital reigns supreme over all other forms of capital, whether human or organizational, ecological or cultural. Those who invest their life and talents in the company have no formal say in the decision, no rights of consultation, and no redress if the promises of the bidder turned out to be false. For this is a model where the basic elements of a mature democracy – transparency and accountability – are absent.

Nearly a hundred and fifty years after the definition of modern company law, firms occupy a strange and contradictory position. Legally they are associations of people to carry out a purpose (which could be anything from the promotion of blood sports to the sale of nuclear shelters), and therefore have responsibilities to act in accordance with their articles of association. In theory, too, the company is a legally distinct entity that is not reducible to any persons including its shareholders (though directors have various responsibilities, such as to use capital for the benefit of members of the company, to maintain the company's capital intact and to abide by various health and safety, factory and employment protection acts). In practice the vast majority of large companies have as their members a floating pool of shareholders, usually dominated by a small number of institutions, and only a single purpose: to maximize the return to shareholders. As one Conservative politician put it nearly fifty years ago:

the human association which in fact produces and distributes wealth, the association of workmen, managers, technicians and directors, is not an association recognised by law. The association which the law does recognise – the association of shareholder-creditors and directors – is incapable of production or distribution.[1]

The Constitutional Debate

The constitution of the economy has only rarely impinged on politics. Innumerable clever and often elaborate schemes for granting employees non-dividend-bearing shares, for ensuring representation on boards, not to mention planning agreements between companies, unions and government, have had little appreciable effect on company behaviour. Few governments have seen much to be gained from tinkering with the source of wealth and employment. So the constitutional debate has focused exclusively on political rights and freedoms and the powers of the state. Given the antiquated nature of much of British law and government, this has been a very necessary process. But even if the very best bills of rights and electoral systems were in place, the agenda of reform would be only half completed. Much of public life – the life of work, money and production – would be untouched. Worse, a one-sided process of reform would further cast in stone the idea that there is a simple division between a public life of politics and an economic life which is treated as purely private. As macroeconomics becomes ever more immune to traditional forms of political influence with the breaking down of trading and other barriers, the harmonization of monetary policy and the globalization of economic activity, any strategy which ignores economic power implicitly accepts that the realm in which people can exercise democratic control will shrink. Domestically too, with a shrinking state and a spreading private sector, any strategy that focuses solely on the formal apparatus of the state is becoming increasingly inadequate to the democratic aspirations of a mature citizenry.

The question of economic rights is nothing new. Socialists have argued for at least a hundred and fifty years that unless political rights are matched by economic ones, persistent inequalities will remain. In the past, however, it was always assumed the state would come to the rescue, defining economic rights and expropriating the private interest of capital and replacing it with the public interest of the community as expressed by the state. The private firm was in this sense a transitional institution, and thus of relatively little interest.

This may be why there has been remarkably little progress on practical alternatives to the capitalist enterprise. The various approaches to reforming private enterprise that have been implemented have all been shown to be deficient. All of the three major alternative traditions have become immobile. The first, the tradition of incorporating enterprises within the state in Morrisonian corporations, has lost most credibility; at best it replicates standard capitalist modes of organization, at worst it degenerates into bureaucratic inertia and vested interest. The result is that few have any remaining principled objection to the passage of public firms at least into employee-owned companies or even into publicly regulated private enterprise.

The second tradition, the long argument about worker directors which caused such bitter dispute as the Bullock Committee deliberated in the 1970s, has also lost its resonance. Within a confrontational corporate culture, the appointment of such directors often simply displaced decision making elsewhere, confused trade unions about their proper role, and certainly gave little real sense of control to employees, since the power ceded was far more a negative one than a positive one. Moreover, the obsession with the board and with power at the centre came to seem less relevant than participation in decisions at the level of the plant or unit.

The third set of traditions has been those of the cooperative movement, which, though successful in small-scale enterprises and through its insurance and consumer wings, has yet to demonstrate how cooperative principles in larger organizations can find a sustainable level of participation for employees. So although the numbers of employee cooperatives has gradually risen, and as many as 60 million people work within various forms of cooperative across Europe, few see them as a viable alternative to the orthodox firm.

Overseas models have also somewhat lost their lustre, notably the Yugoslav model of elected managers, which collapsed as the larger economic system failed to provide any of the requisite disciplines on performance and finance. Similarly, though successful by most criteria, little of the Mondragon experience in Spain has proved transferable to environments which do not share its cultural base. Those looking for models tend to fall back on the more modest example of Germany, with its model of codetermination or *Mitbestimmung* (first introduced in steel and coal to cut back the power of big business, which was deemed to have collaborated too eagerly with Nazism), which gives employees one-third of seats on a supervisory board, or of Swedish-style worker funds for purchasing shares on the stock market, a model which runs the risk of giving far more power to trade union head offices than it does to workers themselves.

So after a century of searching, some of the avenues are closed and some have turned out to be narrow lanes fit only for a few. Pressure for change is now coming not so much from radical reformers in the trade unions and in politics but from within the orthodox business culture. Part of the reason lies in the continuing success of other countries' corporate constitutions that seem to insulate long-term investment, particularly in human capital, from the extreme short-termism of the equity market. A second reason is the continuing success in Britain of less ideological hybrids, such as the John Lewis Partnership, Baxis Heating and Scott-Bader, which have combined employee partnership with a degree of paternalism. A third factor is the new pressure to make firms accountable to society, particularly on environmental issues.

The Economics of the Firm

The Nobel prizewinner Herbert Simon[2] recognized that all economies are made up of organizations, not markets, and that these work well when they foster a sense of common purpose and community, so that workers contribute more than is specified in their work contract. As a result, firms are made up of enabling rules as well as rules of authority, rules which encourage individual responsibility. The economist Edith Penrose went further, recognizing that when people 'become used to working in a particular firm or with a particular group of other men [sic], they become individually and as a group more valuable to the firm in that the services they can render are enhanced by their knowledge of their fellow workers'.[3] In other words, the creation of community is essential to the creation of value and profit, since whereas objective or codified knowledge can be transmitted, collective experience cannot be. The act of working together generates an organizational capital, as important as the human capitals of each employee or the financial capital used to finance equipment or stocks.

Of the two possible models of organization – one authoritarian, where only some do the thinking and others carry out their conclusions, the second democratic, where all think and where thinking and doing are carried out together – it is the latter which is more in keeping with modern economic prerogatives. Thus the rhetoric of modern firms, which is one of lean production and flexibility, emphasizes this democratic model and the 'pride of workmanship' (sic) stressed by W. Deming, the hero of Japanese industry, rather than the discipline and managerial autonomy that became so widespread during the 1980s.

For Britain, such ideas have an archaic ring, for after the paternalistic experiments of the nineteenth century, business effectively displaced community from the firm to the state, which took responsibility for social insurance. The firm's job was simply to produce the wealth for the state to redistribute. The firm therefore ceased to be an interesting political entity, and policy makers turned their attentions elsewhere. This was an historic error, which left much of the world of work untouched by the values of modernity, choice, accountability and transparency. In what follows I set out a three-part agenda for reversing this shift.

Economic Autonomy

Freedom and choice in the world of work depend on having the skills and qualifications to decide the terms on which you enter labour markets. This is rarely the case, not only for the ten million workers without any formal qualifications, but also for many of those who do have some training. Yet this is one area where the individual interest and public interest coincide. For if in the eighteenth century a country's wealth depended on its raw materials of coal and iron ore, in the nineteenth century on its ports and its communications as well as its raw materials and inventiveness, in the late twentieth century human capital – the accumulated knowledge, skill and experience of workers – is the main determinant of the competitive ability of nations and continents. The most modern industries depend on highly skilled, highly motivated and responsible workers, empowered to innovate and make decisions in the application of flexible technologies.

The political implications of this shift in the structure of the economy go far beyond the need for more training, or even the extension of tertiary education to the majority. Rather, what we should be seeking is an agenda for ensuring that citizens have the means for self-realization throughout their life, a set of individual rights as the basis for a learning society.

What might this mean in practical terms? For those in work it would mean entitlements to time off for learning, matched by requirements on employers to train. It would mean a continuing revolution in adult education, to enable employees to control their own skills – extending Open University models to vocational training, and often using the workplace as a place of learning. It would imply a substantial expansion of careers advice and counselling, whether through government or employers or, ideally, through trade unions taking responsibility for negotiating for the individual throughout a varied working life. In the longer run, it would imply an overhaul of the tax and education system to make real the notion of lifetime education and rights to the practical means of self-development. These would be the foundations of economic citizenship and autonomy, understood as control over the means of production – which are now more likely to be in your head or hands than in a machine.

Human Capital – Members of Companies

The second element of the agenda would involve the reform of the corporate sector. As the nature of capital changes, so should the corporate forms which give it legal substance. In the 1990s, capital is no longer scarce in the way that it once was (although it may still be expensive). The only truly scarce resource is mind-power – creativity, skill and knowledge. Even in the most automated industries, the human element is paramount. In automation, for example, it has been estimated that 80 per cent of the potential benefits depend on people's ability to use machines to the full.

The whole structure of company law now needs to be brought belatedly into the late twentieth century. Power comes from the human resources of the company, and from the accumulated experience of the institution as a whole. Consequently, power should be accountable to those who make up the company, and it should ultimately be removable by them, not because 'workers control' should bind back entrepreneurial managements, but rather because any firm that truly rests on the trust and power of its workforces will outcompete one that does not. This is recognized in many of the best firms. But all too often – in both the public and the private sector – habits remain locked in an authoritarian past where managers' right to manage excludes any rights for the employee.

From these issues arises a new agenda of constitutional reform. Whereas most of the conventional debate about corporations is about strengthening the rights of shareholders, tightening the oversight of institutions, increasing independent audits and strengthening the role of independent directors, the essential goal now should be to make it easier for labour to employ capital to its ends rather than vice versa. A first step would be to require consultation of workforces faced by takeovers – in line with the best European practice. A parallel set of reforms should be introduced to make companies more transparent: matching some of the moves in the United States on the publishing of detailed environmental information on inputs and outputs; modernizing accounting to take account of human capital and the other sources of value in the modern firm.

A second stage would be to extend employee decision making – both at micro level and over major strategic decisions. For example, there is considerable scope for extending ESOPs (employee share ownership schemes) to give substantial voting powers to employees.

The third stage of reform would be to bring in a wholesale transformation of company law, to encourage a movement of companies towards new models of human capital companies, where membership is based on investment of time and labour rather than on finance. This should not entail an unrealistic obligation to participate in all decisions, but rather the basic rights of membership of any organization: the right to know, the right to replace, the right to take part in decisions where appropriate. Companies acts could develop a range of new types of legal entity, running in a continuum from the existing company through to fully fledged cooperatives, with a wide spectrum of models in between involving different types of equity, preference share and bond, varying rights to remove capital and varying criteria for accumulating capital (longevity, responsibility, levels of qualification). In general, though, financial investment would increasingly take the form of bonds or preference shares, or equity with tightly defined conditions for the exercise of power. The current hierarchy of capitals, with financial capital at the top, would gradually be overturned.

The Public Interest

The third broad area of reform, to run alongside the extension of citizen rights to human capital, and a reform of company law to give expression to a human-capital-based economy, would involve a reform of what could be called the public interest – the external obligations of firms.

To a large extent, this will have to happen regardless of constitutional change. The deepening awareness of the interrelationships of economy and ecology will require a growing use of ecological taxes, regulations and requirements to act and inform, and a redefinition of directors' liabilities where major environmental damage is concerned.

But there is also scope for going further. One necessary step would be to apply the concept of judicial review to the decisions of large private companies – as Sir Gordon Borrie, formerly Director of the Office of Fair Trading, proposed – so that arbitrary and opaque decisions are banished from modern society. If a major company decided to close a factory, to increase emissions or to dismiss large numbers of staff, it would have to be able to demonstrate that it had taken all relevant factors into account, and acted according to due process, just as is the case with the public sector. One of the responsibilities that would come with the privilege of limited liability would be accountability for the way decisions are made.

A second step would be a tougher articulation of public interest in the economy: through strengthening the powers of the Office of Fair Trading to bust cartels, to protect the rights of small firms in their dealings with larger firms, and to investigate abuses of market power; through new arm's-length agencies to ensure that environmental rules are abided by and that firms meet their obligations to train; through the appointment of public ombudsmen with power to ensure redress where monopoly provision is unavoidable; and through the evolution of new forms of auditing appropriate for the age, which go beyond financial controls to look at the quality of the workplace, of decision-making structures or of waste reduction, through the oversight of a profession rather than the state.

A third set of measures would guarantee a much wider set of rights of economic information. Here a radical new agenda is developing, concerned with the rights of the workforce to corporate information (rights which the European Community Vredeling Directive attempted to guarantee against the intransigence of the UK government), the rights of communities for environmental information (as in a number of US states, notably Massachusetts, where all companies must provide comprehensive information about waste and emissions), and the responsibilities of government to produce impartial, high-quality and – crucially – independent economic information for the use of society as a whole. Here the practice of the present government, of sharply cutting back the provision of public statistical information and confusing the public interest in information with the government's interest, must be reversed.

Conclusions

Fifty years ago, Schumpeter predicted that capitalism would fail because of the loss of motivation that would result as 'dematerialised, defunctionalised and absentee ownership' failed to 'impress and call forth moral allegiance'.[4] Clearly he was wrong: capitalism does survive, even when, for much of the economy, ownership has almost wholly disappeared in a network of electronic transactions. But he was surely right to imply that an economic system can only work to the extent that it calls forth moral allegiance, and that a system where ownership is removed too far from everyday life runs severe risks.

Economic life must adapt to a democratic age: people now expect the right to take part in the decisions which affect them, and find closed, secretive decision making and monopolies of information unacceptable. Employees may not wish to sit on the board, or to be involved in every decision, any more than they wish to be consulted on every bill that passes through Parliament. But the essential elements of democracy – rights to remove, rights to know, rights to choose – are as indispensable in the public firm as they are in the public state. The three broad sets of reforms set out here – concerning the creation of human capital, the reform of companies, and the reformed role of the state – are in this sense only a starting point in the much longer struggle to bring the economy into line with the freedoms and rights which are taken for granted in the rest of social life.

Notes

1   Lord Eustace Percy, *The Unknown State* (1944), quoted in Anthony Crosland, *The Future of Socialism* (Jonathon Cape, London, 1956), p. 266.
2   Herbert Simon, *The Sciences of the Artificial* (MIT, Cambridge MA, 1969).
3   Edith Penrose, *The Theory of the Growth of the Firm* (Blackwell, Oxford, 1959), p. 52.
4   Joseph Schumpeter, *Capitalism, Socialism and Democracy* (Harper, New York, 1942), p. 145.

Part V

Disestablishing the Establishment

16 Making the Civil Service More Accountable

Robert Hazell

I spent 14 years as a civil servant, working in the Home Office from 1975 to 1989. That experience left me with a great deal of respect for my former colleagues in Whitehall, so I begin with some rather defensive remarks about the nature of the Civil Service.

The Civil Service is very large, employing some 600,000 people. All large bureaucracies tend to be regarded as remote, and it is difficult for them to establish a close relationship with their customers. The big banks and insurance companies are also perceived as being relatively distant from their customers. They too are huge organizations, and in recent years they have looked to the public sector for new techniques in increasing their accountability; both the banks and the insurance industry have borrowed from government the device of an ombudsman to investigate customers' complaints.

Second, it is not just in the United Kingdom that government is perceived as being unaccountable; government departments the world over are accused of being over large and remote. What distinguishes the British government from its western counterparts is its excessive secrecy. But again, this is not something which is peculiar to government in Britain: Des Wilson gave examples at the Manchester convention of his accountant and his hospital doctor both refusing to allow him to see his own file. Even the voluntary sector is not immune; there are charitable trusts which refuse to disclose the identity of the trustees. Secrecy is truly the British disease. But in tackling the disease it is right that we should start at the top, with the agencies of central government.

For that we need a freedom of information act. It is depressing to find that the government still maintains that freedom of information is somehow incompatible with a Westminster system of ministerial accountability to Parliament. This was the line adopted by Francis Maude in July 1991, when he claimed that freedom of information 'would undermine the traditional concepts of ministerial responsibility under the Crown and accountability to Parliament' (*The Independent*, 5 July 1991). The experience of the freedom of information legislation in Australia, Canada and New Zealand, ten years old this year, is that freedom of information can work well in countries with a constitution on the Westminster model. Ministerial accountability is not undermined but enhanced by legislation which enables MPs and others to get more background information about government decisions. In itself it is not the panacea which some reformers seem to hope for. Nor is it an automatic guarantee of good government, nor of totally open government. But it is a useful check on the efficiency and fairness of the government machine, and it could symbolize an important change in attitude and principle.

A question people often pose is: how do we ensure that those who carry out public policy owe their allegiance to the public? I believe this is a mistaken way of expressing the present position, or indeed any future aspirations. Civil servants owe their allegiance to the crown. If and when we have a written constitution, they will owe their allegiance to the constitution. In the Institute for Public Policy Research (IPPR) draft constitution, which was presented to the Manchester convention, this principle is written into Article 114.5: 'The first duty of each public service and of every person appointed to a public service is to the Constitution.'

This is not to say that civil servants owe no duty towards the public. They have a duty to be courteous, to be efficient, to be fair and to be truthful. They must show no favours, deal with matters as expeditiously as possible and be as open as possible. That is essentially the agenda of the Citizen's Charter. It seems modest enough. Indeed, it need not require a radical constitutional change. But it would require a major shift in attitudes and a cultural change, particularly in the junior ranks of the Civil Service, who are the front line in terms of day-to-day dealing with members of the public.

It is also part of the agenda behind the hiving off of large parts of the Civil Service into agencies under the Next Steps initiative. The new agencies will be accountable to ministers for their performance, specified in a detailed and demanding contract; but greater management accountability need not necessarily mean lesser accountability to the public. Many of the targets set for service agencies like the Benefits Agency or the Driver and Vehicle Licensing Centre relate to the quality of the service they provide to their customers; and in some areas, like waiting times for driving tests, there have been major improvements as a result.

But treating citizens as customers is not a complete agenda. How can our rights as citizens be improved? There are four practical measures which I would like to see introduced, none of which requires legislation, and all of which could be implemented quickly.

1 *Publication of departments' staff directories*   These are invaluable detailed guides to who does what, giving civil servants' telephone numbers, etc. In Washington, DC, they are freely available to journalists and the like; in London they are still classified. The Home Office staff directory is a restricted document.

2 *Reform of departmental press offices*   These represent a Maginot line which journalists and inquirers seldom manage to get behind. I would like to encourage press offices to transfer inquiries as much as possible to the official responsible for that particular area. When I was a civil servant I used to insist on talking direct to journalists; I would prefer that the briefing came from me rather than playing a game of Chinese whispers through a press officer.

3 *A code of conduct for the civil service*   The First Division Association (FDA – the senior civil servants' trade union) have called for such a code in order to offer guidance in cases like that of Clive Ponting and others where a conflict has arisen between a civil servant's duty to Ministers and his or her duty to the public. I would hope that a code might also be a code of ethics, which would help to resurrect the ethic of the public service as being a serious calling, something of value, and not simply a haven for those who could not make it in the private sector.

4 *Reasons for departmental decision*   I would like to require officials in government departments always to give reasons for their decisions. This would be an important step forward in our administrative law. It is one that has already been made in Australia and New Zealand and in some European countries. It goes to the heart of accountability: a citizen cannot challenge an official decision until he or she knows the reasons which lie behind it.

What about the accountability of the higher Civil Service, in particular for policy making? One reason for the Civil Service being something of a closed world to outsiders is that the senior Civil Service is quite a narrow caste, which would be greatly improved by greater movement in and out. The need for this has been accepted in principle by Whitehall, and last year saw the establishment of the Whitehall and Industry Trust to help promote more secondments; but a lot more could be done. In New Zealand, for example, permanent secretaries are now on five-year contracts.

Finally, I return to the traditional meaning of Civil Service accountability, in the sense of the Civil Service being accountable to the government of the day. I do not subscribe to the conspiracy theory that Whitehall constantly undermines government plans and prevents any radical agenda being implemented. That represented a strong current in Labour thinking, after 1970 and even more so after 1979, with politicians like Tony Benn claiming in their memoirs that the Labour government had been frustrated and undermined by the Whitehall mandarins. At the time the theory sounded plausible; but I believe it has been completely exploded by the experience of the Thatcher government. In the years since 1979, Whitehall has showed itself to be a very flexible and highly effective machine in doing the government's bidding. Opponents of the Conservative government may not like the result, but it is undeniable that the Civil Service did respond to ministerial commands and has implemented the Conservative government's agenda, even when many civil servants disliked that policy.

In conclusion, I would say there is no quick fix or simple solution to achieve greater Civil Service accountability. Government departments are huge and complex organizations and, like Gulliver lying on the sands of Lilliput, they need many different lines of accountability to pin them down. These include Parliament, the press, the courts, tribunals, select committees, auditors and ombudsmen. All have an important role to play in ensuring that the Civil Service is responsive both to its political master and to the needs of the people.

(provision for continuous audit and regulation) rest on assumptions about how quality performance can be achieved and sustained. All this is conveniently summarized in the Government's latest white paper about the role of the Civil Service, 'Competing for Quality'.

What the alternative democratic project, now being promoted by people across the centre and left of British politics, needs is a similar consistency of approach: not just a theory of greater accountability in government but a practice, grounded in experience, with demonstrable application to a new-style public service. To aim for less will be to risk repeating the mistakes of the immediate post-war period, when implementation of the welfare state reforms was compromised by the style in which they were implemented and managed.

It is not sufficient simply to assert that the new right's reforms have failed to deliver. We must be able to advocate convincing alternative strategies. In order to achieve a new settlement that will last, all sorts of institution in our society, not just those on which Charter 88 has hitherto focused attention – the two houses of Parliament and the judiciary – are going to have to change fundamentally, not only in composition, but in working style and culture. What is still generally called the establishment, which has ridden the waves of the new right's 'radical' reforms with practised skill, will have to be permanently disestablished. It cannot be too early to start thinking seriously about how this difficult job is going to be done. How can we create open, accountable structures free of class privilege, racism, sexism and doctrinal extremism (of any kind) and ensure they are equitably and efficiently managed?

This is not to say that criticism of the failures of the past decade is irrelevant. The pervasive influence of what the free market Institute of Economic Affairs likes to call the 'new consensus' is one of the obstacles in the way of devising clear alternatives. Part of the job has already been done for us. For example, the difficulty of demonstrating that any substantive general benefit has resulted from the privatization of public services is clearly reflected in the government's desperate efforts during the 1992 general election campaign to persuade the electors that they did not have the least intention of applying yesterday's miracle remedy to the National Health Service. The prospect of improved accountability through wider share ownership, once widely touted, has lost much of its gloss, as the proportion of shares owned by individuals fails to rise and company chairs shrug off shareholders' attempts to hold them to account for policy decisions. Moreover, customer complaints are proving to be less effective in practice than market theory has always maintained. The disproportionate profits recorded, in mid-recession, by the newly privatized utilities – and the salary increases awarded to their chairs and senior executives – have increasingly come to be seen as abuses of their monopoly position at the expense of the consumer. Insult has been added to the injury inflicted by continual price rises by the squandering of money on the trappings of corporate image – most notoriously, British Telecom's ridiculous 'pied piper'.

These basic weaknesses are sufficient in themselves to discredit the uncritical adoption of market-based remedies.But a different approach will be needed when existing centres of monopoly power (both traditional and newly created) are being dismantled. What are the alternatives? A reversion to the status quo ante is clearly unacceptable. Simply to set up an ideal image of a well-planned and well-resourced (and altruistic) public sector will not do. It is not practical politics. Nor is it desirable. Public sector bureaucracies have a built-in tendency to degenerate, unless checked, into cartels whose main objective is defence of producer self-interests.

If the job is to be done properly, we need to go back to first principles. I propose three points of departure: first, clarification of objectives; second, determining the scale at which to concentrate reform; and third, establishing a new style of management for and delivery of public services, and ensuring that it pervades all aspects of every service.

Objectives

Are constitutional reformers seriously interested in reviving a strategy for equality? The emphasis on rights, entrenched and justiciable, implies that they are. But decentralization of power does not necessarily produce equality of outcomes. If anything, the tendency will be the other way, with resources and competence varying widely between different areas and agencies. Privatization has had similar consequences. One of the declared objectives of introducing market disciplines into the public sector is to create losers as well as winners. These losers will almost certainly be those whose rights are least secure. Privatization of prisons (and now, almost unnoticed, police forces) puts rights at risk in a particularly sensitive area. But simply reversing or checking the process is not sufficient in itself; the overall objectives of policy need to be identified clearly. Reform requires careful thought about the devices that can ensure standards are maintained across different groups and geographical areas, and quality services continue to be delivered, while securing public involvement in planning and delivery of those services. The cost factor may be crucial: there is a potential trade-off between democracy and efficiency at work here. If so, how is it most effectively resolved?

Scale

One of the explanations given for the past failure of public service agencies was size (excessively large) and the level at which decisions were taken (needlessly high). One simple solution is subsidiarity: delegating responsibility with linked resources to the lowest point at which services can be effectively managed. This will usually, but not invariably, be either at local authority level or below (the neighbourhood). This form of decentralization works well in other societies, but it needs the support and confidence of those for whom the service is intended. Proper means of securing accountability is one answer; involvement in implementation is another – through expansion of the role of local voluntary and community groups, for example. However, effective devolution will depend in large measure on changes taking place in the third area.

Style

The style in which public services are managed in future will certainly be different. This is partly the result of developments over the past decade, which have brought some much-needed improvements in the responsiveness of public sector workers to the needs and preferences of users. Some of these changes – especially those that have taken place within the Civil Service – are due to the adoption of procedures from the market. Some are the results of direct intervention by the government, in legislation and through the activities of the Audit Commission. Other reforms have been internally generated within local government, which received little credit for them. In fact, most of the innovations associated with empowering of citizens have their origins at local rather than national level. Still others stem from the widespread introduction of new technology and the opportunities this provides – especially in information technology and data processing. Assuming personal responsibility for quality of service, as exemplified in the identification of the individuals concerned, has been another important development. More imaginative management which provides greater scope for enterprising individuals and rewards successful innovation is also a necessary part of this process.

But many of these policies have been compromised by the economic context in which they have been introduced. Market values have been imposed in programme areas where they sit uneasily with the style and objectives of the service. The limits on the effectiveness of such approaches emerge at once in situations where resources are scarce. There is no particular merit in wearing what Roy Griffiths calls the 'fixed smiles of arctic winter' when unable to offer practical assistance to meet pressing need. The new enabling style dwindles into simply 'saying no nicely'.[2]

Nevertheless, the government are determined to press ahead with the approach set out in John Major's Citizen's Charter, which is based on the principles of 'improving choice, value and accountability'. A new government department has been set up, with the explicit objective of ensuring that charter objectives are met across the whole range of public services. With a full term in front of them and the very evident personal commitment of the prime minister, it is clear that these objectives will be energetically pursued. But the means proposed are deficient in several crucial respects. Apart from the crucial weakness on resources, the focus throughout is on individual remedies. As Peter Kellner argues:

Market mechanisms – or their substitutes, in the form of redress when things go wrong – will deal with some problems in the public services but not others. They are less useful for running those services that we do not use now, but may one day, or those that we do use, but wish to influence, even when they are going well; or those we want to enhance, because they add to the quality of life of our neighbourhood or nation – in short, those services we cherish not just as consumers, but also as citizens. (*The Independent*, 19 July 1991)

So the cut-price, partial remedies of the Citizen's Charter and its mixed menu of marginally useful or wholly irrelevant devices will carry us only a short distance – and not always in the right direction. Some of them may assist individuals as consumers of services, but they have nothing to offer on their rights as citizens, especially when these are being obstructed or denied through structural discrimination on grounds of race, gender or disability. A revitalized public sector has to address these questions not as marginal issues, but as central questions which determine the extent to which services can meet needs across the board.

Conclusion

These issues are not bolt-ons, to be considered after the structural reforms for which Charter 88 and associated lobbies are rightly pressing have been introduced. They require answers now, because they account for much of our current dissatisfaction with the existing state of affairs and are crucial if we are to find a remedy. If they are neglected, the potential for a decisive shift towards accountable government and public services will be compromised.

Notes

1 Austen Albu, quoted in Elizabeth Durbin, *New Jerusalems* (Routledge, London, 1985), p. 274.
2 Roy Griffiths, 'Does the Public Service serve?' in *Public Administration*, 66 No. 2 (London, 1988), p. 196.

18 Reform of the Judiciary

Sally Hughes

The reform of the judiciary is virtually axiomatic in the movement for constitutional reform. A written constitution, entrenched in English law, would confer the enhanced power on judges not only of interpreting its provisions but also of ruling on the constitutionality of parliamentary legislation. But Parliament's will, theoretically the democratic outcome of the electoral process, could not, it is said, be controlled by an essentially undemocratic, unaccountable judiciary: particularly not the present judiciary, which has, for a variety of poorly explained reasons, been found wanting. Under the new constitution, the separation of powers would somehow be manipulated into a continuous loop of democracy. And many worthy and intelligent minds have recently been engaged in designing the institutional machinery, usually of a judicial commission, accountable to a parliamentary select committee, to achieve this.

What *is* the current debate on the judiciary? There is no consistent or theoretically based body of thought on the social and political role of the modern judiciary, although classical nineteenth-century constitutional theory is often cited to locate judges as a 'limb' of the constitution. Such as it is, the current debate contains two schools of thought: the technocrats' and the ideologues'. This chapter is less an attempt at a formulation than an erection of signposts in a debate which floats through and around the speeches of the Great and Good, and the pages of the 'intellectual' mass media.

The Judiciary as Technocracy

The term 'technocracy' is used to here to denote a view of law as an objective science. Technocrats believe that judging is a technical task, that judges are objective and brainy, their role being simply that of applying and interpreting given law. Technocrats play down the role of judicial creativity, explaining it as the inevitable result of adapting law to individual cases.

According to this view, there is no doubt that the present judiciary (or indeed any 'qualified' judges) are capable of fulfilling rightly and correctly the will of the people. After all, judges have ultimately, albeit a shade reluctantly, allowed, in the Spanish fishermen's case (*R.* v. *Secretary of State for Transport ex parte Factortame*) that European law potentially overrides parliamentary legislation.

Technocrats' overriding principles are derived from the abstractions of constitutional law. Chief among these is judicial independence: a term that embraces many things and is closely linked to the concept of judicial authority. Judicial independence means freedom from (partisan) political pressure. It entails indefinite appointment and relatively high financial reward in order to insulate these most upright public servants from prejudicial enticements. It includes, and here it shades into the notion of authority, peremptory powers to control proceedings in the court in which they preside and a large say in the definition of legal procedure generally. In a sense, it also includes the wigs and paraphernalia that reify judicial personae. The authoritarianism of judges derives from technocratic assumptions about the inherent rightness of the application of law as science and justifies the insulation of so intellectual a process from any non-legal demand.

In the scandal that erupted in the 1990s over the miscarriages of criminal justice of the 1970s, a few technocrats argued (mostly in private, because it conflicted with decency and morality) that the preservation of judicial authority would have justified the continuance of the injustice: that what was viewed almost as inevitable technical error need not be allowed to disturb the notion of judicial infallibility or undermine judges' unanswerability.

Then there is the reaction of technocrats to the increasingly well-documented lunacies of the judicial backwoodsmen to consider (who have said, to cite a few examples, that a rape complainant was 'contributorily negligent' in hitching a lift late at night; that the crime of an offender who committed a sickening rape and assault was mitigated by the fact, apparent only to the judge, that his victim, calm and composed in court, had suffered 'no great trauma'; that the male partner suffers more than the woman from miscarried pregnancy). Such statements have done much to undermine public confidence in the judiciary. Yet according to many technocrats the sins of individual judges, such as they are, are mere aberrations: only particular individuals are old and sexist and out of touch.

For other technocrats, who acknowledge that fundamental problems exist, the solution is twofold: the superficial acceptance of the new generalities ('accessibility', 'openness', 'confidence') with the reinforcement of the old technocratic principles.

Lord Taylor, the Lord Chief Justice, draws a distinction between 'independence' and 'remoteness' (Guildhall speech, 15 July 1992). He has encouraged the judges to go on television so that, in certain respects, they may be shown to be similar to, and to understand the concerns of, ordinary people. He has also encouraged them to dabble in public committee and consultative work outside the courts. What is meant by this openness is not an accounting to or involvement of wider influences in the work of the judiciary, rather a kind of explication to the unknowing, ignorant public of the essential rightness of the existing system.

Second, Lord Taylor asserts that, in the light of loss of faith in the criminal justice system, judges must restrict themselves to their technical function and not stray into judgement of factual issues reserved for the jury by adding their own gloss to the summing up of factual evidence (Guildhall speech). This is in fact disingenuous. Judges necessarily have an important role to play in interpreting the facts of any case in the light of the law. In criminal trials, where juries are involved, judges also determine questions of admissibility of factual evidence, and once evidence on the borderline of admissibility is allowed before the jury, the jury then faces a similar dilemma, albeit couched in different terms. While Lord Taylor mentioned the need for 'vigilance' on the part of trial and appeal court judges, he made no elaboration of their role at this crucial interface between fact and law. Such a policy is essentially protective of judges, and correspondingly throws a greater load of responsibility on to jurors.

Thus Lord Taylor's construction of the judicial role, perceived as the application of technical legal knowledge, suggests greater rather than less isolationism. Of course neither of these tactics – encouraging judges to make carefully managed media appearances or to retreat behind the law – impinges on the essential authoritarianism of the judicial function.

Ideologues: Judges as Class Representatives

This line of thought is more simply stated. It has been refined and reduced by criticism and academic debate since Professor John Griffith first published *The Politics of the Judiciary* in 1977. This work tapped into, perpetuated and stimulated the conventional wisdom that judges drawn from a narrow social base unconsciously bend their apparently objective legal decisions to serve the interests of their own class – the ruling class.

The manner in which legal academics have debated this has been in the self-defeating and methodologically suspect legalistic tradition of analysing written judgements of politically sensitive cases by the judges of the court of appeal and House of Lords. The result is that for every judgement demonstrating class bias, another can be produced from which an opposite or neutral outlook can be inferred. A related problem is that this too closely resembles traditional jurisprudence itself, which is characterized by the, at times, almost random sifting of precedent to find 'authority'.

Ideologues are therefore diametrically opposed to technocrats. Basic legal technique according to technocrats is to reach a 'result' via induction from legal precedent – applying a 'science', in other words, blind to the possible outcome. Many ideologues believe, on the other hand, that judges make their decision first and then find the legal reasoning to justify it. (Some judges have openly subscribed or admitted to this approach.)

More than that, ideologues assert that judges are in effect subjective manipulators of legal ideas to incorporate social or political values normally assumed to be innately conservative and government oriented. Where government policy is uncertain, as in Conservative Party ambivalence to Europe, then judges reflect this.

Ideologues view the 'hidden' judicial agenda as undemocratic. The process is either unconscious or not explained by judges themselves. It does not exist in a context in which it can be debated, argued with or challenged; judges cannot be engaged on the subject and tend in any case to deny it.

Judicial Reform and a Bill of Rights

For this reason, many ideologues join constitutional reformers in favouring some means of choosing judges that is democratically validated, and, above all, removed from the secretive, gossipy enclaves of the Lord Chancellor's Department and circuit messes (the Lord Chancellor, Lord MacKay, has endorsed a move towards 'fair, efficient and open' methods of judicial selection, but only in the traditional context, in which he alone decides). At the same time, they would also want to employ social, cultural and political values within this redefined process of appointing judges and ultimately in the definition of their tasks, particularly those concerning civil rights.

First, they point to the American system of political validation (by a committee of the Senate) of the appointment of supreme court judges (by the US president) in which nominees to the court have their intellectual and ideological baggage opened up and hung out for public inspection. This can involve analysis of their in-court and out-of-court statements and academic work for just the type of ideological biases documented by Griffith. In recent years, notably in the case of opposition to the nomination of Clarence Thomas, even a complaint about a long-past work relationship was given a hearing in these proceedings.

Second, drawing on experience, particularly in the US federal courts and the European Court of Human Rights, they advocate bringing in evidence on the social and economic impact of the application of the law into the legal process.

From the point of view of ideologues, a bill of rights inevitably raises the stakes in the judicial reform debate, given that judges would be given wide powers to interpret human rights law. Indeed, many ideologues are opposed to a bill of rights because they believe, in the light of American experience, that an illiberal or right-wing judiciary would simply subvert the rights enshrined in such a bill to class interest. Even if we were able to reform the judiciary swiftly enough, they feel it would still be undesirable to give judges what is an essentially political role in deciding our rights.

By way of contrast, leading reformer Anthony Lester QC does not think a bill of rights should wait on judicial reform. Pointing to the duty of judges to interpret Britain's existing anti-discrimination legislation, Lester contends that the British judiciary is already engaged in the process which others contend they cannot adequately perform.

Judging or Judges?

Lester is, however, concerned to see a more representative bench. In fact, there is almost universal subscription to the view that a more socially representative bench would be a good thing, bringing not only greater enlightenment on social issues but a richer mixture of skills. But little thinking has gone into the relationship between judging and the judges. To what extent does the composition of the judicial personnel affect legal and democratic processes? All we have had thus far is a sterile argument between those who say that through the ages, clever, white, male jurists, by the objective and independent application of legal science, have secured as much social justice as might clever jurists of any other genetic make-up, and those like Professor Griffith who argue that the class background of the top judges has resulted in class-biased judging.

We have already seen the weakness in both these cases, namely that they rely on a selective interpretation of leading judgements – technocrats dismissing patterns of illiberal or sexist judgements as isolated incidents and ideologues ignoring any evidence that contradicts their viewpoint. What is also clear is that both suffer from a fixation with the top tier of judges to the exclusion of the rest of the bench. The judiciary is like an enormous, tiered wedding cake: with a great base of lay magistrates, steeply and sharply rising to the group of formally dressed figures of the Law Lords at the top – visible and much scrutinized. For those obliged to eat this cake, it is the unseen contents of the layers, at first sight smothered in icing and decoration, which are the most important. Once the judiciary is fully examined from the bottom up rather than from the top down, as I propose to do here, the case for reform of personnel becomes more apparent and the debate begins to emerge from the sterility of traditional legal discourse.

Magistrates

Britain has a relatively small full-time professional judiciary and possibly the most multifarious range of lay, legal, full-time and part-time judges in the developed world. Two thousand professionals, in the sense of those having a legal qualification, are dwarfed numerically by the 29,440 part-time lay magistrates. Legal issues in a magistrate's court are effectively decided by a paid professional court clerk.

There is no doubt that the Lord Chancellor is anxious to recruit a more socially broad-based magistracy – Lord MacKay has boasted on several occasions that modifications to the recruitment process have resulted in a fast recruitment of black magistrates that is rapidly correcting the imbalance between the proportion of ethnic minorities in the population and on the bench. In the past decade, the proportion of women magistrates has risen from 40 per cent to 45 per cent (a continuing minority that seems inexplicable given the comparatively greater freedom of women from the labour market). But the underlying values behind this attempt to create a more representative bench are unexplained and unrefined. Is social representativeness secured only by crude characteristics such as race and gender? That there is no coherent approach to these issues is evident from the arbitrary and honorific system of nomination, which still favours the educated, well-connected and successful of any social milieu.

Since the magistracy is essentially a democratic institution, perhaps its members should be democratically elected, under a system that would prevent the intervention of sectional interests. At the moment, sectional interests are present in the sense that political parties and local interest groups are among the main sources of nominations.

Another important issue is how far the cherished local discretion of magistrates conflicts with the trend, expressed through parliamentary legislation, towards certainty and standardization in sentencing. Which is the most democratic (a question that also applies to professional judges)? Benches all round the country adopt widely differing practices. Does democracy demand that the same style and standard of justice should be available to all defendants, regardless of where the offence charged was committed? And does accountability mean that benches which, for instance, deny legal aid to above-average numbers of defendants should be obliged to justify their policies?

What is the role of the deceptively labelled 'clerk' to the magistrates, whose advice on questions of legal aid and law generally informs so much of the magistrates' work? In France, such a functionary would doubtless be a member of the professional judiciary. He or she would be obliged to conform to judicial disciplines and also be eligible to climb the judicial career ladder.

Professional Judges

At least half of professional judges are in fact part-timers: 1,240 lawyers (usually barristers) who have been in professional practice for 16 to 18 years (longer for women practising in London and the south east) and who serve as assistant recorders and recorders. By sitting for four weeks a year, they together handle 25 per cent of crown court cases and just over two per cent of high court cases. Ultimately they may join the 470 full-time circuit judges, only a handful going to the high court and beyond.

The under-recruitment of qualified women as recorders has been detailed.[1] Causes can be located partly in the culture of recruitment, which is one of masonic secrecy and old-school-tie support. But my inquiry also revealed inhibitions operating on women which are deeply imbedded in the culture of both branches of the profession, and which derive in turn from the treatment of women in the wider society. The presence of significant numbers of women in the male world of the law is still so new as to be regarded as a concession. Provision for maternity and family responsibilities is possibly the lowest among any of the professions, due to the lack of structured employment among lawyers.

Professor Griffith's assumptions about 'class' interest failed to take into account both the impossibility of a truly 'working-class' lawyer and the ideological divergence within the professional middle class. He also ignored the intrinsically different experience of women in all levels of society. Feminism among women lawyers is not, as some have suggested, simply bourgeois careerism. Women interact differently with the law. On the bench they are capable of claiming the law for women.

For a long time, lord chancellors argued that women could only be recruited according to their proportion in the qualified legal professions: anything else, it was implied, would amount to positive discrimination and be tainted by the suspicion that the additional proportion would not have been appointed according to the same criteria as men and would thus be less well qualified. When research showed that women were being under-recruited and only recruited (in the case of that half of the profession working in the south east) with apparently better credentials than men, the argument was clinched. The numerical increase in assistant recorders in the 18 months since the original data analysis consists of 55 per cent women.

It therefore seems that, stimulated by the exposure of empirical evidence and public opinion, the existing system is capable of producing the desired result. Why reform?

First, the process of judicial appointment is still poorly accounted for and inadequately informed. Instead of trumpeting such a progressive year of recruitment, the Lord Chancellor's Department has kept quiet about it. This fact alone demonstrates the tension still existing between the 'democratic' ideal expressed by the present government and much of the public (that women should be present in much greater numbers on the bench), and the fear of the existing legal establishment that women will feminize (that is, lower the status of) and otherwise dilute the true nature of the judiciary. It also shows how easily policies can be made and broken behind closed doors.

The technocrats are wrong to view the process of judgement as a functional and technical one. If that were the case, then the field would have been abandoned to women long ago. In the vast bulk of society's contact with the law, both civil and criminal, the judge represents a social authority beyond that of enunciator of the law.

Women on the bench would no more propagate ideological feminism than appeal judges dispense ideological capitalism. But they would make a difference to the judicial process. The strongest effects would be felt in the lower courts, where the quality of justice is critical for democracy, because facts – more properly, social realities – dominate the work.

Democratic Validation of Judicial Appointments

To return finally to the issue of reforming the way we appoint our judges, it is clear that we need some form of democratic vetting or confirming of judicial appointments. We need a wide-ranging debate about how this might be done. In some states of the United States, certain judges are elected by going to the hustings and attracting the popular vote. In others, a nominative process involves screening by a wide and public committee system.

Simon Lee has argued that the operation of the US Bill of Rights and Supreme Court has led to a huge industry of pressure groups, mobilizing great resources of expertise and media campaigning to secure test-case victories in the supreme court and influence the outcome of the judicial nomination process.[2] In other words, they hijack the process for those who might otherwise have asserted their will, leaving the inarticulate at the margins.

Would this be the result of a British judicial commission and bill of rights? Before we take the plunge, we must work to discover, elucidate and understand the relationship between judging and judges, and judges and society.

Notes

1   Sally Hughes, *The Circuit Bench – A Woman's Place?* (The Law Society, London, 1991).
2   Simon Lee, *Judging Judges* (Faber, London, 1988), chapter 23.

19 Making the Police More Accountable

Sarah Spencer

There is wide agreement that the 'tripartite' system of accountability established by the 1964 Police Act, in which responsibility for the police was divided between the Home Secretary, chief constables and local police authorities, has broken down. There is also some agreement that the unique division of local responsibilities in the act, which reversed the traditional relationship between appointed officials and councillors – so that the councillors advise but the chief constable takes the decisions – is wrong in principle and practice.

Many of the decisions taken by senior police managers are political in the sense of involving a choice of priorities, conflicts in the allocation of resources, and having unequal effects on different groups in society. They involve choices in the style and method of policing (such as whether to use task forces and the degree of involvement with other agencies); the acquisition of technology and rules about its use; the deployment of officers and other resources to particular geographical areas, and the emphasis put on certain offences; the value placed on and rewards given for certain kinds of behaviour by junior officers, and the degree of sanction for misdemeanours; and so forth.

Such decisions should be taken by a fully elected body, not police authorities as presently constituted with one-third magistrates, two-thirds councillors. If we are seeking constitutional change in order to decentralize power, ensure that government is accountable and transform the country's subjects into citizens, the accountability of the police must be on the agenda. When the Institute for Public Policy Research drafted its constitution for the United Kingdom, designed to be entrenched as the United Kingdom's fundamental law, it would not have been appropriate to include detailed institutional arrangements for police accountability. We did, however, seek to entrench four basic principles:

1 Parliament and the assemblies (when established in Scotland, Wales, Northern Ireland and the English regions) must enact procedures making each police force accountable to elected representatives for the performance of their functions.
2 Selection procedures must be adopted which would ensure that adequate numbers of candidates of both sexes and diverse racial, religious and social backgrounds are considered for appointment.
3 An independent body must be established to investigate malpractice by police officers with the power to investigate, regardless of whether a complaint has been received.
4 Individuals who have suffered as a result of such malpractice should receive effective redress including compensation.[1]

There is plenty of scope for amending or adding to these basic principles, the significance of which is that they would be entrenched in the constitution and binding on Parliament and the assemblies. The most difficult task, however, is devising the detailed institutional arrangements in statute to establish an acceptable and workable relatonship between appointed officials (the police) and elected representatives at the national and local level. As in other public services (witness the well-publicized conflict in Stratford school in 1992 between the elected governors and the professional headteacher), it is not easy to find a legislative framework which ensures that elected representatives determine policy and priorities without interfering in the day-to-day running of the service, or enabling individual politicians to exercise an improper personal influence over officials' decisions. Some would-be police reformers in the United States have looked wistfully at the insulation of our police from political control as preferable to the corruption and bias within their own system.

When considering the detailed institutional arrangements which would be appropriate, a number of points should be considered. First, before we try to change the system we must understand the present balance of power in the tripartite structure. It is well known that the limited power of police authorities has been eroded over the last ten years, for instance by:

the abolition of the radical Metropolitan authorities and their replacement by
joint boards made up of district council nominees, through which the Home
Secretary effectively controls the resources of almost half the police
strength in England and Wales;

developments during the miners' strike of 1984–5, during which police authorities found that they had no control over the huge expenditure which
their chief constables were incurring as a result of mutual aid from neighbouring forces;

the 1987 Northumbria Police Authority case, in which the court of appeal ruled
that plastic bullets could be supplied to chief constables from a central
source if their police authority refused to purchase them;

most significantly, the way in which central government grants are used to
control police expenditure, a system which the Audit Commission criticizes
as undermining the authority of police authorities: 'A balance has always
been struck between the interests of central government, local government
and the police service itself. But the balance has now tilted so far towards
the centre that the role of local police authorities in the tripartite structure is
significantly diminished. Accountability is blurred and financial and management responsibilities are out of step';[2]

a significant change in the style of Home Office circulars from one of guidance
('it is to be hoped that chief constables will consider . . .') to one making
clear that resources will not be made available if the desired behaviour is
not forthcoming.[3]

It is often assumed that these developments have increased the autonomy of chief constables. The reality is that it is the Home Office
which has increasingly assumed control; not direct control, for which
the Home Secretary would have to be accountable to Parliament, but
indirectly through its control over grants, its veto on appointments to
senior posts and its increasingly didactic circulars, and by proxy
through Her Majesty's Inspectorate of Constabulary and the Association of Chief Constables. Robert Reiner is right to conclude that a
'major obstacle to reform is the shadowy and secretive way in which
the police are controlled and organised' and that the Home Office has so
effectively moved towards a national force that 'overt nationalisation
would ratify rather than transform the status quo'.[4]

One of the major tasks in devising a new structure is to decide which
decisions should be taken at the national, force and local level, and what
are the most appropriate means of democratic accountability for decisions at these levels. The way in which the structure of decision making

develops over the next decade will be influenced by a number of factors, including the proposed reform of local government; the pressure to develop national police units to deal with certain kinds of crime; and the impact of growing European union.

No decision has yet been taken on the future structure of local government, but the abolition of county councils, the tier of government of which police authorities are a part, is one likely outcome. The government has denied that the proposals in the Department of Environment 1991 consultative paper on the future of local government would lead to changes in the structure of police accountability under the Police Act, but it is difficult to see how substantial changes could be avoided if county councils were abolished. The most likely outcome would be that the government would propose the creation of more joint boards of district council nominees under a degree of Home Office control (as in the former Metropolitan areas) with a further consequent loss of local accountability.[5]

The limits of Britain's local police force structure have led to calls for the police to be reorganized on a national or regional basis. The fact that the investigation of the Lockerbie disaster fell to the smallest force in the country highlighted one anomaly in the existing structure, for which amalgamation into larger forces is not, however, necessarily the answer. One alternative solution has been the development of ad hoc national arrangements to deal with crimes which extend beyond regional and national boundaries, most recently the National Criminal Intelligence Service. Such developments highlight the danger of ad hoc arrangements, which may be necessary but are subject to inadequate supervision because the police force is not organized on a national basis and there is no democratic control at that level, Parliament having been given (or taken?) no role.

While the government talks of decentralizing police decision making within forces in line with Audit Commission recommendations – and has announced a year-long review in May 1992 to consider this and related management issues – a greater pressure is being felt to centralize decision making. This comes not only from the need for national operational units but from Europe. The uncertainty over the course which future European cooperation will take and the pace of change is reflected in the ad hoc arrangements which have so far been made to corrdinate UK policy with that of our EC (European Community) partners. The existence of 43 separate forces in England and Wales alone in itself creates difficulties when harmonization of policy and cooperation on operations are being discussed. At present, it is not clear who is taking responsibility for policy in relation to Europe, different bodies being represented on different committees while some are excluded – for example, the Royal Ulster Constabulary, despite its obvious interest in and experience of one of the issues under discussion, terrorist violence. If the lack of accountability for developing policy is a concern, the democratic deficit which would accompany any move towards a pan-European force would be far greater. Yet such a force is already on the agenda for some in key policy positions. Roger Birch, chief constable of Sussex, speaking at a seminar at Bramshill Police College, envisaged 'one set of laws common to Europe with freedom for the police to operate without judicial restriction across the whole of a united Europe. In this Utopia it would be possible to develop a European police strategy and indeed to establish a truly European Federal Police System.'[6]

A further point should be considered. In recent years there has been a drive to cut public expenditure while improving police performance. The Home Office has demanded all kinds of new facts and figures from forces seeking extra resources, including detailed job descriptions, activity analysis and performance review. As in the health service, where the motivation for these quality-of-service initiatives has in part been to give managers the ammunition to take on the health professionals, the driving force in policing has been the desire to provide the Home Office with the ammunition to take on chief constables. As a result, there has been a definite increase in internal, managerial accountability. The police and the Home Office call this 'accountability'; but it is important that we do not confuse it with the kind of external, democratic accountability which we are seeking.

The 'haemorrhage of public confidence in the police'[7] has led senior officers to stress the service role of the police and to a commitment to adjust policing priorities to meet those of the public. As the chairman of the Association of Chief Police Officers put it, 'there is a need to go to the community to determine their policing priorities, balance them against our professional judgement, and agree a new level of expectation.'[8] This matches police authorities' own interpretation of their role in recent years. While research has shown some variation in the extent to which they now use their powers, there is a definite emphasis on crime prevention and community relations issues rather than, for instance, seeing themselves as a voice for those with views on police priorities and methods. One of the means which is used to obtain the views of the public is opinion polls. As Reiner points out: 'The recent General Election should have sensitised us to the problems of opinion polls and market research techniques, on which the police increasingly rely, as compared to the electoral process as a means of registering public opinion.'[9]

Were there to be a constitutional change which put responsibility for determining policy and priorities in the hands of the public and their representatives, the kind of information which is being generated by the performance review process would no doubt be as useful to them as it is now to Home Office officials and Her Majesty's Inspectorate. However, the indicators which are chosen to measure performance depend on the objectives which the police are expected to achieve. If the public were to have a greater say in determining those objectives, the performance indicators might need to be revised in turn.

Finally, in devising our new system, the most difficult issue to resolve will be this: how can we ensure that the needs and priorities of *all* sections of society are heard and become influential in the decision-making process? What means can we use to ensure a voice for the young, for black people, for travellers, for the homeless, and for other groups who are not represented on most local authorities and certainly not on the majority of police authorities which, it should be remembered, are Conservative controlled? Simply handing control to local police authorities as presently constituted will not end the mismatch between police and public priorities or bring to an end the kind of malpractice which has led to the dramatic fall in public confidence.

Devising a new institutional structure will not in itself bring about adequate change. There are many other interrelated issues which need to be tackled – management style, the discipline system, training and masonic loyalties, to name but a few. We must indeed question whether the whole system is designed to achieve the right balance between apprehending the guilty and protecting the innocent. In relation to constitutional change, however, our primary objective must be to put responsibility for the police firmly in the hands of democratically elected and fully representative bodies. The people will thereby have the means to ensure that the other necessary reforms are undertaken. Whether they choose to do so will then be their decision.

Notes

1 *The Constitution of the United Kingdom* (IPPR, London, 1991).
2 Audit Commission Police Paper No. 6, *Footing the Bill: Financing Provincial Police Forces*, June 1990, p. 6.
3 Charles Clark (Chief Superintendent), *Policing*, 7 (1991).
4 Robert Reiner, *Chief Constables* (Oxford University Press, Oxford, 1991), p. 8.
5 Barry Loveday, *Police and Government in the 1990s: The Impact of Proposed Local Government Reorganisation on the Structure of Police Forces in England and Wales*. Birmingham Polytechnic Institute of Public Policy Management Occasional Paper No. 3 (1991).
6 Roger Birch, seminar at Bramshill Police College, February 1991.
7 Aptly so called by Robert Reiner in his inaugural lecture '*Fin de Siècle* Blues: Policing Post-modern Society', London School of Economics, May 1992. Public respect for the police fell from 83 per cent in 1959 (reported in the report of the Royal Commission on the Police (1962), Cmnd 1728) to 43 per cent in 1989 (MORI poll for *Newsnight*).
8 Michael Hirst, seminar at Bramshill Police College, February 1991.
9 Reiner, '*Fin de Siècle* Blues'.

20 The Media and the Constitution

Jean Seaton

Would a written constitution together with a bill of rights improve the British mass media, make them worse, or leave them little affected? Like many aspects of our political system, the principles underlying political communication have scant recognition in law. The biggest obstacle to enshrining them in a constitutional clause is deciding what they are.

It might be said that the basic functions of political discussion in newspapers and broadcasting are to inform and to express: to tell the public what it needs to know, to reflect public demand, and to organize, anticipate and even at times lead public opinion. It might also be said that the objective of journalism should not merely be to relay the facts, but to act as a channel between expert and lay person, to translate specialist knowledge into accessible common sense.

It is obvious to everybody, however, that the framing of such principles has little to do with the actual experience of most editors, producers, journalists, readers and viewers. The real function of all but a tiny segment of mass communication is entertainment. A raised legal or constitutional status for the press and broadcasting might successfully erect ramparts around the service provided to a small minority, while doing nothing to protect or improve the quality of the media diet of the overwhelming majority.

Clearly there is a persuasive case for the constitutional entrenchment of media rights, and it has been greatly strengthened over recent years. The long period of one-party domination in Britain encouraged a level of government interference which would not previously have been tolerated. The Thatcher era was scarred with politically inspired attempts to circumvent press freedom: the Northern Ireland broadcasting ban; the injunctions against the publication of *Spycatcher* by the retired intelligence officer Peter Wright; the prosecution of Clive Ponting and Sarah Tisdale for passing information which in other, more liberal systems would have been freely available; a series of interventions against the makers and producers of television documentaries (of which *Real Lives* and *Death on the Rock* were the most notable examples). These have all contributed to a climate of cynicism in which politicians have ceased to expect freedom of expression to be respected. If an informal system has broken down, it is certainly arguable that a formal system, with precise and enforceable rules, is required to take its place. A freedom of speech clause might render illegal many of the infringements of press and broadcasting freedoms against which there is at present no redress. It would have the additional advantage of reducing the gagging effect of Britain's quixotic libel laws, in so far as they affect matters of legitimate public interest.

Such a clause might be invoked to prevent the recent, disgraceful practice of packing the Board of Governors of the BBC with political stooges and using them not to defend the corporation's independence but to secure its compliance. It might prevent the effective waiving of monopoly legislation to permit the takeover of newspapers by pro-government proprietors. But above all – and this is the crux of the constitutionalists' case – the existence of a carefully defined right to freedom of speech and expression would provide a benchmark against which all controversies involving alleged infringements could be judged. Thus the duties and obligations of the media could reasonably be raised in a discussion of the future of the level of BBC licence fees. At the same time, an agreed clause might be expected to become the starting point of all debate about the media and (so some would contend) the continuing guarantor of a fundamental liberty.

Many of these arguments stem from a disturbing sense of traditional freedoms slipping away. Such a feeling underlines the need for reform. It does not, however, ensure that reform will work. The real difficulty with a 'freedom of speech' clause is not that it is wrong, or even that it is inadequate. It is rather that it concentrates on a small corner, while ignoring the whole crumbling edifice; and in so doing, fails even to recognize the possible side effects.

There are a number of points involved. First, challenging governmental actions in the courts on constitutional grounds is almost always easier for the rich than for the poor. This has certainly been the experience of both the United States and Germany, where the 'right to be heard' is much more frequently invoked by individuals and interests with the resources to fight costly court actions than by those that lack them. In the United States, corporations have successfully begun to claim the speech rights of individuals through appeals to the constitution in the courts. Second, the existence of a constitutional provision does not in itself ensure that it will be respected. Where it runs against political or corporate interest, these interests will do all in their power to evade it.

Third, enshrined constitutional clauses are necessarily short, while the range of possible threats to the media freedom is infinite. Even the best-drafted clause cannot cover every situation, and – as the history of constitutions everywhere shows is liable to a wide range of possible interpretations, varying over time, including many which the constitution makers may never have envisaged. When the founding fathers enshrined freedom of speech in the American constitution, it is unlikely that they imagined that it would be taken to mean that any upper limit on election spending by candidates or their backers is unconstitutional – which is how the US courts have recently interpreted the clause. The borderline between 'unlimited freedom of speech' and 'unlimited freedom to pay for advertising and propaganda' is not one that is easy for even the best constitutional lawyers to define.

Beneath the pressure for a free speech clause lies a presumption that the problem in political communication is one of censorship and muzzling, as in the fashionable 'right to reply' which was taken up by media unions in the 1970s and 1980s. According to this view, any group or organized interest suffering a criticism which it deemed unfair should be able to reply in kind and insist that its riposte is given equal prominence to the original attack. This could be invoked to give less powerful or affluent groups a voice. Such a right, however, does nothing to ensure that anyone will listen. For in a highly competitive market-place of media entertainment, sensation and debate, only the most powerful and innovatory messages of protest will stand any chance. If the issue is how to produce better, more responsible, more inquiring, more honest political media, the answer is not to be found in constitutional reform but in the nature of the industries and how they are managed.

The pressures against responsible and challenging political journalism have little to do with formal rules and are unlikely to be affected by any change in them. A constitutional clause might, perhaps, inhibit the grosser forms of political bias and might even increase the opportunities for contrary opinions to be expressed. But it would not make bad good, or render the acceptable shocking, or make the complacent challenging, or turn the banal into something imaginative. It would not remove the intense commercial pressure on newspapers and broadcasting companies to go for the cheapest, the least problematic, and choose material that is likely to reach the biggest audiences of the right social profiles. To take one obvious though little-discussed example: children are big consumers of television, they are the most impressionable section of the audience, and deserve the best, in terms of the social, political, creative and broadly educational quality of what they are served up. Yet without the restrictions posed by public service regulation, the resources devoted to children's broadcasting are proportionately tiny because, though numerous, children are not big enough spenders to generate the advertising revenue which makes it possible to raise standards and make better programmes.

It is not the state of the law, but the commercial environment, which provides the American public with a wide range of low-budget, low-quality television channels whose political content, such as it is, is blander, less controversial and less directed at contemporary problems that do not have an instant entertainment value than in Britain. It is not the law in Italy – where there is both a written constitution and a radically deregulated television service – that provides the hapless Italian public with a remorseless diet of packaged American news reports, old American movies, American and Japanese cartoons, and low-cost chat shows; that has rendered careful documentary making, or serious television drama, not so much endangered as extinct species. In Britain, the Conservative government's most powerful weapon against broadcasters has not been political censorship but the determined assault on the financial basis of public service broadcasting.

In some circumstances the state is undoubtedly the enemy of media freedom, but it can also be a friend, and one whose role it would be foolish to exclude. State interference is one thing, state regulation and state patronage another. Who would not agree that the involvement of the state in broadcasting over a long period in Britain has been beneficial, in terms of the variety, quality and political 'balance' of what the public has been provided with, and that the nation has been better served than would have been the case if the media had simply been left to the ravages of the ungoverned market? So successful has been the history of state involvement in broadcasting that, at a time when all the pressures favour disengagement, a powerful argument can be made for applying lessons learnt from radio and television to newspapers and introducing similar forms of regulation to curb the wilder abuses of the popular press.

Thus the emphasis of the constitutional reformers may be in the wrong place. They should be less concerned with guaranteeing opportunities to publish, and more with stimulating creativity and innovation; less concerned with formal rights, and more with the structures which encourage good quality. The preoccupation with real or supposed state censorship may be misplaced. The recent history of countries where censorship has been absolute for generations does not suggest that people can easily be brainwashed. The citizens of democratic countries are far less handicapped by the comparatively minor restrictions to freedom of speech that exist than by the suffocating pressure of triviality and blandness which rampant economic forces are permitted to produce, often in the name of political freedom.

In short, as far as the media are concerned, two cheers for a written constitution with a freedom of speech clause. To enshrine such a right, which is widely seen as important, would at least encourage people to cherish what they have taken for granted. But it would only begin to solve the problems of inadequate and deteriorating political communication. 'Where there is much desire to learn,' wrote Milton, in *Areopagitica*, 'there of necessity will be much arguing, much writing, many opinions.' Constitutional reform may provide formal protection for the freedom of the media, but there is no substitute for a difficult, complex and bold policy initiative to improve quality.

Part VI

Devolution, Sovereignty and Interdependence

21 The Necessity of Regionalism

David Byrne

There has been an episodic debate throughout the twentieth century about the desirability and/or possibility of regional government in the United Kingdom.[1] Commentators[2] have often remarked that this debate has confused and compounded a number of different themes: the desire for national identity in Scotland and Wales; the desire to devolve power from an inefficient and remote centre; the desire for the democratization of that substantial element of devolved administration which does exist; and the desire for a system of subnational administration and/or government which can deal with the very substantial interrelated issues of land use and economic planning. That all these things matter is true, but my argument is that the last three – the desires for devolution, democratization of devolved powers, and the achievement of an effective system of land use and economic planning – are in reality interrelated aspects of one problem. This can only be understood by recognizing the interaction of social geography with political history in this country in the last quarter of the twentieth century.

The easiest way to do this is by giving a brief account of the origins of my own interest in the issue of regional government. In the early 1980s I was course tutor to a Workers' Educational Association class discussing the social consequences of economic change on Tyneside, and then a member of the Tyne and Wear 2000 Group which developed from that class. We first identified the nature and extent of de-industrialization in our conurbation, and the potential (and now only too real) social consequences of division, deprivation and disorder which would flow from that process. We then considered what might be done, and rapidly concluded that there was a major deficiency in the machinery of government. The administrative level which might handle these problems was missing. Even the metropolitan county council, itself wholly inadequate for the task for the reasons so trenchantly identified by Derek Senior in his Minority Report of the Royal Commission on Local Government,[3] was about to be abolished. There was a deficit of administration and a massive deficit of democracy.

We faced a central government which had no real political interest in our region. It had little to lose in electoral terms and no real prospect of any electoral gain. The Tories could afford to ignore the north, and to a considerable extent Labour could afford to take it for granted. The Thatcherite political programme disadvantaged us (and other similar regions based on manufacturing industry) in two interrelated ways. First, there was a very clear and open hostility to planning mechanisms as part of the machinery of government. Decisions were to be left to markets. Second, the economic future of the United Kingdom was seen as 'post-industrial'. Employment in manufacturing would be allowed, or even encouraged, to decline. The future lay with services and in particular with information services, which were part of the financial markets located in the south east.

This was a very important shift from the corporatist political culture of the United Kingdom in the post-war years. For all its undemocratic character, and success at incorporating and neutralizing the objectives of organized labour, the corporatist culture had recognized that full employment depended on economic modernization achieved through a system of planning. In the post-war years, planning was seen as a way to solve problems. After 1979, planning was seen as problem-creating. So far as we were (and are) concerned, full employment was a sine qua non in a free society. If mesoeconomic planning of investment, as well as Keynsian macroeconomic management, was necessary to achieve and maintain it, then planning we must have. The alternative was to exclude many of our fellow citizens from the right to a decent life.

So planning is necessary for economic purposes, and I will outline why the regional level is crucial for such planning. However, the economic cannot stand alone. The major planning process which is necessarily local in our sort of society is land-use planning. It is impossible for a central authority to have the information necessary to take detailed land-use decisions. Some devolved system must be devised. That, though, is an argument for local government; the argument for some higher level comes from two things. The first is the need to integrate residential and transport development at a level of administration which takes in much more territory than that of the level which is best suited to the delivery of local services. This is an argument for Senior's city regions and had particular significance and force for the greater south east. The second is the necessary relationship between land use and investment planning (in both physical and human capital) as part of a mesoeconomic planning system for modernization, and for the sustaining of a viable environment. This is a matter for the regional/ provincial level. The rest of this chapter will outline the necessary form(s) of regional government and argue that if these forms are not democratic and federal, then they will not work.

I think that the right approach is to start by analyzing the facts of social geography, the requirements of functional effectiveness and the conditions of democratic viability in relation to one another, to let the outcome of this analysis determine the appropriate scale of units for groups of related functions, and then to see what principles of social organization best fits the needs thus ascertained and the practicalities of the transition to a new structure.[4]

That seems excellent advice for anybody looking at this issue. I propose to follow it, and in so doing will in part, if not quite completely, agree with the man who gave it. In so doing I will work as he did, not from the centre down but from the local up, and agree very largely that local government which delivers the ordinary services of the state – housing, environmental health, school (but probably not post-16) education, personal social services, primary health care and the general run of secondary hospital-based services – should be at a scale which allows for direct ordinary contact and be unitary in form. However, there is a level beyond that, which is the level of serious strategic land-use planning in a society where work, consumption and residence are dissociated in space – where many of us do not live where we work or shop and do not shop where we work, and so on.

To resolve this problem, Senior argued for 35 new city region authorities, in addition to the existing Greater London, which had been excluded from the Royal Commission's remit. What we got was the farthest possible remove from Senior – a two-tier shire system and conurbation authorities with boundaries tightly tied to existing built-up areas. This has created considerable problems for strategic planning and for much else as well.

Senior recognized that the city-region was too small a unit for all planning matters. There was also a need for a subnational but supracityregion provincial level: 'A provincial strategic plan is needed because of the interlocking character of the problems – spatial, social and economic – that arise on the province scale and can be comprehended and resolved only by an agency looking at the province as a whole.'[5] Senior and the majority of the Royal Commission on Local Government agreed on the need for a province system, but disagreed on numbers. They argued for eight English provinces; he for five. The issue for both was primarily administrative. There was a task to be done and there must be a body to do it. Senior was inclined to the view that the body should be nominated rather than directly or indirectly elected. His solution was corporatist.

The authors of the minority report of the Royal Commission on the Constitution took a different view.[6] For Senior the problem was one of administrative failure; for them it was a potential failure of the democratic system. They concluded that:

the essential objectives of any scheme of constitutional reform must be:
(a) to reduce the present excessive burdens on the institutions of central government.
(b) to increase the influence on decision making of the elected representatives of the people.
(c) to provide the people generally with more scope for sharing in, and influencing, governmental decision making at all levels.
(d) to provide adequate means for the redress of individual grievances.

In our view all the evidence makes it clear that it is just as important to achieve these objectives for the people in the different regions of England as for people in Scotland and Wales.[7]

In the detail of their proposals, Crowther-Hunt and Peacock adopted Senior's recommended five English regions, in addition to Scotland and Wales, and argued for a reform of the UK constitutional system so that the second chamber would have a considerable regional element in it, following their general principle of interlocking the levels of government. They allowed for a continued nominated, and even possibly hereditary, element in the second chamber, but argued that it made simple sense to imitate the German example and make the second house an indirectly elected House of the Regions drawn from the provincial governments. Senior's memorandum to the Royal Commission on the Constitution is worth quoting here:

if the structure of local government is not radically reorganized – in particular if conurbation authorities on the GLC model are substituted for the broad city-region units on which all members of the Radcliffe-Maude Commission were agreed [and that is exactly what did happen] – elective provincial authorities will become the only hope for the future of English local democracy and for planning as a local government function.[8]

So, in the early 1970s there was a congruence of arguments about functional efficiency and democratic process around the notion that elective provincial assemblies within England were a good idea. The recommendations of Crowther-Hunt and Peacock were clearly feder-alist. In particular, the interlocking principle made the provincial (re-gional) level relatively immune from revision by the national level of government. There was a wide and informative debate about the finan-cial and fiscal basis of regional government, and about the relationship of national and regional economic and fiscal policy. That is important, but there is not the space to go into it here. Instead we need to look at what has happened since.

John Tomaney and Neil Turnbull sum it all up very well in their paper,[9] which has been circulated as a background document to the recently established Campaign for a Northern Assembly. They argue that since 1979 the commitment to a market-led, financial-services-dominated, south-eastern oriented set of economic policies has starved the United Kingdom's manufacturing sector, which is disproportion-ately important to the country's peripheral regions, of investment resources, and generated a climate operating against industrial modernization and development. Indeed, contrary to formal claims of non-intervention, central government created a network of non- (and often anti-) democratic agencies to impose this model where elected local government would not. Particularly important here were the urban development corporations (UDCs) exemplified by the Tyne Wear De-velopment Company, which is actively enforcing the handing over of key river-fronting industrial sites to non-industrial residential and other service developments, and doing so in the face of a collapsing property market.

All this is happening whilst unemployment, and perhaps even more importantly underemployment, have become the reality of life for a large proportion of the population. This is particularly the case for those people who have had the bad luck to enter the labour market since the combination of international recession and specific UK economic mismanagement have so devitalized our employment base. We have passed a disproportionate part of these costs to our children. The effect has been the creation of a divided society, divided not so much on ethnic grounds (although ethnic minorities have done badly, as have women) as by a combination of the effects of class and age. The young working-class poor have been written out, not least by a systematic removal of their citizenship benefit rights. This is what lies behind the riots of 1992 on, for example, the Meadowell Estate in North Shields, immediately adjacent to the strategic deep-water industrial site of Whitehill Point, which the local UDC is attempting to develop as the yuppie marina and leisure-based village of 'Royal Quays'.

This assault on industrialism and full employment is not merely economic. It is also cultural. The response of Scotland to Thatcherism seems to me to have had as much to do with the way in which people whose personal lives and family experiences had been based on industrial life in all its aspects were deeply affronted by the glib dismissal of this as outmoded and irrelevant as with any specifically nationalist sentiment. It is certainly the reason why the north of England produced an absolute majority vote for Labour in April 1992, and why the Tories have been so reduced as a force in local government in places like Tyne and Wear.

To sum up, in the 1990s we have a situation which is a good deal worse than that which existed when the issues of subnational government were systematically examined in the late 1960s and 1970s. We have a serious economic mess, a disaffected and disorderly poor, an increasingly powerless local government system which was reorganized in England and Wales (although not in Scotland) in a way which meant that key functions could never be properly carried out, and a central government which prefers to rule though nominated appointees. Where do we go from here?

Imitation here may be the height of flattery, but it also seems to be good sense. Before the Germans lost their good sense and imposed a western system on their very different reacquired east, they had a system of government and administration (and in principle and often in practice still do) which provides us with a model of how we might do things. Germany has been very successful as a society, precisely because it got the administrative mechanisms for mesoeconomic planning right, and its democracy and civil society have been greatly enhanced by the assigning of these mechanisms to democratic control by the

Laender government, at least so far as German citizens are concerned.

The problem with our society is that in its modern history political power has always been centralized, and in the twentieth century economic power has likewise become centralized, both through the extended economic role of the state and through the concentration of capital. A federal democratic system of provincial governments in England, Wales and Scotland is vital. Without it we will have economic stagnation and social disintegration.

It is also now clear that this fits the future towards which Europe is moving. The achievement of direct representation at the European level by the German Laender prefigures the development of the Europe of the regions. Furthermore, there is evidence that regionalism has popular appeal. The Royal Commission on the Constitution found in the early 1970s that the development of regional government was the most popular option for political and administrative change, and that this approach was almost as popular in England as in Scotland, and more popular in England than in Wales.[10] The most recent evidence comes from an ICM poll for *The Guardian* reported in October 1991. Then 42 per cent of respondents favoured English regional governments (almost exactly the figure of twenty years earlier), 28 per cent did not know and 29 per cent were against. As yet, this wish for regional government in England has not been turned into a demand, but that is a matter for organization and action.

Notes

I should like to note the helpful comments of Simon Partridge and John Tomaney on an earlier draft of this piece. I have not always followed their advice, but I was very glad to have it.

1 See J.C. Banks, *Federal Britain* (Harrap, London, 1971); B.W. Hogwood and M. Keating (eds), *Regional Government in England* (Clarendon Press, Oxford, 1982).

2 M. Keating, 'Whatever happened to regional government?', *Local Government Studies*, 11 (1985), pp. 111–22; U. Wannop, 'Do we need regional government?', *Regional Studies*, 22 (1988), pp. 438–46; G.W. Jones, 'Against regional government', *Local Government Studies*, 14 (1988), pp. 1–11.

3 D. Senior, 'Royal Commission on Local Government in England and

Wales 1966–9, Vol. II: Memorandum of Dissent', Cmnd 4040-I (HMSO, London, 1969).

4   Ibid., para. 18, p. 5.

5   Ibid., para. 485, p. 141.

6   Crowther-Hunt and Peacock, 'Royal Commission on the Constitution 1969–73, Vol. II: Memorandum of Dissent', Cmnd 5460-I (HMSO, London, 1973).

7   Ibid., para. 10, p. xiv.

8   D. Senior, 'Written Evidence, Vol. 8: England: Royal Commission on the Constitution' (HMSO, London, 1972), p. 219.

9   J. Tomaney and N. Turnbull, 'Taking the north into the twenty-first century: the case for democratic reform and economic renewal' (1991).

10 Crowther-Hunt and Peacock, 'Royal Commission', ch. 2.

22 The European Constitution

Richard Corbett

Whatever the final outcome of the Maastricht process, Britain is already part of a wider system of government which takes decisions, including binding legislation, affecting a substantial area of public policy making. This tier of government has its own written constitution in the form of the Community treaties, which spell out the areas of Community competence and the decision-making procedures to be used in each case. They also entrench certain specific rights such as equal pay for equal work, non-discrimination on the grounds of nationality, and the four 'economic freedoms' to trade across frontiers. In this system, decision-making is dominated by governments of the member states, giving it a traditional intergovernmental appearance, but the effects of those decisions when taken in the form of Community legislation (which overrides national legislation) are more federal in character.

It is important neither to underestimate nor to overestimate the impact of the European Community (EC). It should not be underestimated because it does impact – and if Maastricht is ratified will impact still further – on a whole range of policy areas: virtually all aspects of economic policy, the environment, consumer protection, public health, regional development, vocational training, agriculture, transport, fishing, external trade, overseas development aid, monopolies and mergers, research and technological development, educational exchanges and many more. President Delors once estimated that up to 80 per cent of economic and social legislation in our countries would be of European origin by the late 1990s – even if it is only half as much, it would still be a considerable proportion of public policy making.

On the other hand, this impact should not be overestimated. Far from being a centralized 'superstate', the Community is very much in the hands of its own member states, any one of which can bring the Community to a grinding halt if it so chooses. The 'Brussels bureaucracy' is in fact smaller than that of most local authorities in Britain. The EC budget represents some 3 per cent of total public expenditure (the other 97 per cent being national, regional or local) and a mere 1.2 per cent of gross domestic product. It has no access to instruments of coercion or force. Important areas are kept outside of the Community's legal framework and handled purely on intergovernmental basis (notably foreign affairs and police cooperation). Finally, what it may do is strictly limited to the areas spelt out in the Treaty, implementation of which requires the support of at least a qualified majority (71 per cent of the votes) – and for some items unanimity – of the ministers in council. These are ministers of *national* governments, who are not normally keen to limit their own margin of manoeuvre more than necessary. Community policies are initiated and administered by the commission (appointed by national governments), voted on by the council (composed of ministers from national governments) and, if there is a dispute, ruled on by the court of justice (composed of judges appointed by national governments). The idea that Brussels is able to impose policies on reluctant member states and to 'invade the nooks and crannies' of national life without the consent of the member states is preposterous.

Indeed, the current debate on subsidiarity is a red herring, designed to overcome resistance to the Maastricht Treaty by Tory right-wingers in Britain and floating voters in Denmark. This is not to say that there is no genuine concern among the public about excessive interference from Brussels – but this concern had been fuelled to a large extent by governments themselves trying to blame the Community for unpopular decisions or trying to resist the application of Community legislation that they had previously agreed to. The case of the Winchester by-pass is illustrative: far from trying to dictate the route that this road should follow, as it was specifically accused of doing by assorted ministers and newspapers, the Commission merely wished to verify that the United Kingdom had undertaken an environmental impact assessment, as required under Community legislation. The British government, which in the early days of the Maastricht negotiations had argued that the failure of certain states (viz. unreliable Latins) to apply Community legislation was one of the key issues that should be addressed, suddenly switched to backing subsidiarity (whose incorporation into the treaties was first advocated by the European Parliament) as a way of resisting Community legislation that was inconvenient to the government.

Subsidiarity may be a bogus argument, but there are none the less problems with the way the Community adopts legislation. First, legislation is enacted, at the end of the day, by a vote behind closed doors in the EC Council of Ministers. The council is the only legislature in Europe to adopt binding legislation behind closed doors, failing to respect the fundamental democratic principle that the public should be able to see how its representatives voted. At present, not even the minutes are published.

It would merely take a revision of the Council's internal rules of procedure, which can be done by a simple majority, to change this situation. It would not require treaty amendment. Nor would it be necessary to make *all* Council meetings public – when it is deliberating on foreign policy, for example, it could continue to meet behind closed doors. However, when acting as the Community's legislature voting on a proposal from the executive commission, it should meet in public.

Even if it were to vote in public on Community legislation, though, there would still be a problem with the council remaining the principle legislative body of the Community. For the council is nothing less than the executive branches of our member states meeting collectively. National ministers, by coming together in the Community, can adopt legislation without it necessarily being subject to the approval of either the European Parliament or of national parliaments. They could even adopt in this way legislation that they were not able to force through their national parliament. This again flies in the face of a fundamental democratic principle. Ministers alone should not be able to enact legislation without the approval of an elected parliament.

The Treaty of Maastricht goes some way to remedy this situation by introducing a co-decision procedure, so that legislation requires the approval both of the European Parliament and of the council. However, the importance of this innovation is limited in two ways. Firstly, the procedure is in fact weighted in favour of the council in that if, after two readings each in council and Parliament and following a conciliation procedure, there is still no agreement between the two bodies, council may act unilaterally, and its text will become law unless it is overruled within six weeks by the European Parliament acting by an absolute majority of its members. Secondly, the procedure will apply only to a limited proportion of Community legislation – somewhere between a quarter and a third. For the rest, the European Parliament will be involved through a variety of procedures (cooperation, consultation), which give it certain rights of amendment but fall short of rejection. Maastricht is a step forward, but an insufficient one.

The role of national parliaments can also be strengthened. The Treaty of Maastricht encourages this through an annexed declaration in which member states undertake to ensure that 'national parliaments receive Commission proposals for legislation in good time for information or possible examination'. The declaration also calls for the stepping up of contact between national parliaments and the European Parliament through the granting of the appropriate reciprocal facilities, and a separate declaration invites the European Parliament and national parliaments to meet together as a conference or 'assizes'. In fact, irrespective of the Maastricht Treaty, the question of national parliamentary control over their own government's representative in the Council of Ministers is a matter to be settled between each parliament and its government. At present a wide variety of procedures exist in the various member states, ranging from the Danish Folketing, whose specialist committee meets with ministers before and after the Council meetings, to three national parliaments (Belgian, German and Greek) which have set up specialist committees composed, on a parity basis, of MPs and MEPs. In the United Kingdom, recent procedural changes in the House of Commons have enhanced scrutiny, but there is much that could still be done. Nevertheless, it should always be borne in mind that separate scrutiny by 12 different national parliaments each of an individual minister who is just one member of council is bound to be inadequate, and must be complemented by the strengthening of the European Parliament referred to above.

A further problem with council is the unanimity provision still applicable to many areas of legislation. Although few would question the need for unanimity for constitutional matters such as treaty amendments or the accession of new member states, or for any enlargement of the Community's field of competence, it is quite another matter when it comes to managing of policies that *have* been attributed to the Community. If, as is the case, it has been agreed to deal at Community level with certain aspects of environmental policy, and Community legislation lays down certain standards for emission levels of particular pollutants, it is nonsensical to make any changes to those standards dependent upon the unanimous consent of each member state. Such a veto means that all the other states are potentially hostage to the position of just one. It is the dictatorship of the minority. In such a situation, the lowest common denominator tends to dominate – the last thing one wants in environmental policy. If a matter is to be subject to Community-level regulation, the rule of the majority – albeit a qualified majority – must apply.

Transparency, clarity and democracy – these are elements that are still to be found in insufficient qualities in the Community, despite improvements offered by Maastricht. There is still an agenda for constitutional reform at Community level. Its importance and urgency can only grow as the Community takes on new responsibilities. The new intergovernmental conference scheduled, by Maastricht itself, for 1996 is an opportunity for change, as are the enlargement negotiations which should take place before then. Let us hope that they do not chase red herrings.

23 Democracy and Globalization

David Held

A decision to increase interest rates in the attempt to stem inflation or exchange-rate instability is most often taken as a 'national' decision, although it may well stimulate economic changes in other countries. A decision to permit the 'harvesting' of rainforests may contribute to ecological damage far beyond the borders which formally limit the responsibility of political decision makers. A decision to build a nuclear plant near the frontiers of a neighbouring country is a decision likely to be taken without consulting those in the nearby country (or countries), despite the many risks and ramifications for them.

Decisions such as these, along with policy decisions on any number of other pressing issues, are usually regarded as falling within the legitimate domain of authority of a sovereign nation state, periodically accountable to its citizens. Clearly, such a state may consult with other states about particularly pressing matters and, indeed, may form modes of collaboration and organization to counter transnational problems. The framework of European Community (EC) institutions, or the recent attempt to create an international regime to manage the reduction of the use of carbon fluorochlorides, are obvious cases in point. Yet, despite these highly significant developments, the norm remains that policy and law are matters first and foremost for individual nation states and their citizens.

Even the democratic critics of existing structures of state power tend to think of the problem of political accountability today as above all a national problem. State structures are, they hold, insufficiently responsive to their citizens. In various forms of participatory democracy, or in contemporary models of the democratization of state and civil society, the emphasis is placed on making the political process more transparent and intelligible, more open to and reflective of the heterogeneous wants and needs of 'the people'.

The problem, for defenders and critics alike of the existing state system, is that regional and global interconnectedness contests the traditional national resolutions of policy problems and outcomes. The very process of governance is escaping the reach of the nation state. National communities, and their governments, do not exclusively make and determine decisions and policies for themselves. Further, decisions made by quasi-regional or quasi-supranational organizations such as the EC, the North Atlantic Treaty Organization (NATO) or the World Bank diminish the range of decisions open to given 'majorities'. The idea of a 'national community of fate', a community which rightly governs itself and determines its own future – an idea at the heart of the modern state itself – is today deeply problematic. Although this will be no surprise to those nations and countries whose independence and identity have been deeply affected by the hegemonic reach of empires, old and new, it remains a surprise to many in the West.

Developments putting pressure on the nation state are often referred to as part of a process of 'globalization' – or, more accurately put, of 'western globalization'. Globalization in this context implies at least two distinct phenomena. First, it suggests that political, economic and social activity is becoming world-wide in scope. And, second, it suggests that there has been an intensification of levels of interaction and interconnectedness within and between states and societies which make up international society. What is new about the modern global system is the chronic intensification of patterns of interconnectedness mediated by such phenomena as the modern communications industry and new information technology; and the spread of globalization in and through new dimensions of interconnectness: technological, organizational, administrative and legal, among others, each with its own logic and dynamic of change. Politics unfolds today, with all its customary uncertainty, contingency and indeterminateness, against the background of a world shaped and permeated by the movement of goods and capital, the flow of communication through cable, airways and space satellites, and the passage of people.

Globalization places questions on the agenda which go to the heart of the categories of democratic thought. The idea that consent legitimates government and the state system more generally was central to both seventeenth- and eighteenth-century liberals as well as to nineteenth-

and twentieth-century liberal democrats. For instance, liberal democrats focused on the ballot box as the mechanism whereby the citizen periodically conferred authority on government to enact laws and regulate economic and social life.

But the very idea of consent, and the particular notion that the relevant constituencies of voluntary agreement are the communities of a bounded territory or a state, become deeply problematic as soon as the issue of national, regional and global interconnectedness is considered and the nature of a so-called 'relevant community' is contested. Whose consent is necessary, whose agreement is required, whose participation is justified, in decisions concerning, for instance, AIDS or acid rain or the location of a nuclear plant? What is the relevant constituency? Local? National? Regional? International? To whom do decision makers have to justify their decisions, and to whom should they?

Territorial boundaries demarcate the basis on which individuals are included in and excluded from participation in decisions affecting their lives (however limited those decisions might be), but the outcomes of these decisions most often 'stretch' beyond national frontiers. The implications of this are profound, not only for the categories of consent and legitimacy but for all the key ideas of democracy: the nature of a constituency, the meaning of accountability, the proper form and scope of political participation, and the relevance of the nation state, faced with unsettling patterns of national and international relations and processes, as the guarantor of the rights and duties of subjects.

How should democracy be understood in a world of independent and interdependent political authorities? The problem of democracy in our times is to specify how democracy can be secured in a series of interconnected power and authority centres. For democracy involves not only the implementation of a cluster of civil, political and social rights (freedom of speech, press and assembly, the right to vote in a free and fair election, a universal and free education and so on), but also the pursuit and enactment of these rights in a complex, intergovernmental and transnational power structure. Democracy can only be fully sustained in and through the agencies and organizations which form an element of and yet cut across the territorial boundaries of the nation state. Democracy will result from, and only from, a nucleus, or federation, of democratic states and agencies.

The principles and requirements of democracy, therefore, have to be enshrined in, and enacted within, national and international power centres, if democracy is to be possible even within a delimited area alone. Democracy within a nation state requires democracy within a network of intersecting international forces and relations.

In short, the possibility of democracy today must be linked to an expanding framework of democratic states and agencies to embrace the ramifications of decisions and to render them accountable. I refer to such framework as 'the cosmopolitan model of democracy'. How should it be understood? What are its institutional requirements?

In the first instance, the cosmopolitan model of democracy presupposes the creation of regional parliaments (for example, in Latin America and Africa), and the enhancement of the role of such bodies where they already exist (for example, the European Parliament) in order that their decisions become recognized, in principle, as legitimate independent sources of international law. Alongside such developments, this model anticipates the possibility of general referenda of groups cutting across nations and nation states, with constituencies defined according to the nature and scope of controversial transnational issues. In addition, the opening of international governmental organizations to public scrutiny would be significant.

Hand in hand with these changes, the cosmopolitan model of democracy assumes the entrenchment of a cluster of rights in order to provide shape, and limits, to democratic decision making. This requires their enshrinement within the constitutions of parliaments and assemblies (at the national and international level); and the expansion of the influence of international courts so that groups and individuals have an effective means of suing political authorities for the enactment and enforcement of key rights both within and beyond political associations.

In the final analysis, the formation of an authoritative assembly of all democratic states and agencies – a reformed General Assembly of the United Nations, or a complement to it – would be an objective. Agreement on the terms of reference of an international democratic assembly would be difficult, to say the least. Among the difficulties to be faced would be the rules determining the assembly's representative base. One country, one vote? Representatives allocated according to population size? Would major international functional organizations be represented? But if its operating rules could be agreed, the new assembly could become an authoritative international centre for the consideration and examination of pressing global issues such as food supply and distribution, the debt burden of the Third World, ozone depletion, and the reduction of the risks of nuclear war.

If such a development sounds like fantasy, it is equally a fantasy to imagine that one can advocate democracy today without engaging with the range of issues elaborated here. If the new emerging international order is to be democratic, these issues have to be confronted, even though their details are, of course, debatable.

The implications for international civil society of all this are in part clear. A democratic federation of states and civil societies is incompatible with the existence of powerful sets of social relations and organizations which can – by virtue of the very bases of their operations – systematically distort democratic processes and hence outcomes. At stake is, among other things, the curtailment of the power of corporations to constrain and influence the political agenda (through such diverse measures as the public funding of elections, the use of 'golden shares' and citizen directors), and the restriction of the activities of powerful transnational interest groups to pursue their interests unchecked.

If individuals and groups are to be free and equal in the determination of the conditions of their own existence, there must be an array of social spheres which allow them control of the resources at their disposal without direct interference from political agencies or other third parties. At issue is a civil society that is neither simply planned not merely market oriented but, rather, open to organizations, associations and agencies pursuing their own projects, subject to the constraints of democratic processes and a common structure of political action.

In short, in the context of globalization, democracy requires a rethinking of both the nature and scope of the modern nation state and the form and structure of the central forces and agencies of international civil society. Two distinct issues arise: first, recasting the territorial boundaries of systems of accountability so that those issues which escape the control of a nation state – aspects of monetary management, environmental questions, elements of health, new forms of communication – can be brought under better control. Second, it is necessary to articulate political institutions with the key agencies, associations and organizations of international civil society so that the latter can become part of a democratic process – adopting, within their very modus operandi, a structure of rules and principles compatible with those of democracy. Of course, such developments might take years, if not decades, to become entrenched. But 1989 showed that political change can take place at an extraordinary speed, no doubt itself partially a result of the process of globalization.

Part VII

Building a Culture of Citizenship

24 Democratic Innovation in Scotland

Isobel Lindsay

In 1886 a Scottish academic said to Benjamin Jowett, 'I hope you in Oxford don't think we hate you.' Jowett's reply was, 'We don't think about you.' Not thinking about Scotland is no longer a sufficient response by England to its neighbour. This is not just because Scotland is discontented and politically troublesome, but because Scotland offers a new opportunity to break with constitutional conservatism in the United Kingdom.

Constitutional issues have a vitality and centrality in Scottish politics which is not true of other parts of the United Kingdom. This is largely because they have been linked to feelings of national identity. But there may also be factors which stem from a longer tradition of concern for democratic rights. In the nineteenth century, for example, Scottish society was deeply divided over the right to democratic self-determination in the Presbyterian church.

The 1980s intensified the feeling of being deprived of democratic rights. Scotland, with its different legal, educational, administrative and local government systems, with a wide range of separate state and voluntary organizations, with a four-party system, with a substantially different press, was being governed by a political party representing less than a quarter of the electorate. This situation was aggravated by the government's determination to push ahead with a radical right agenda in Scotland despite its questionable legitimacy.

The clash of political cultures was more intense in Scotland than elsewhere. The Thatcherite brand of competitive individualism never came into fashion. Collectivist values continued to be broadly acceptable across social classes. It was within this political context that an initiative was taken to try and change the nature of the constitutional debate and to broaden its range. The debate on the Scottish government issue had gone on for over twenty years in its modern phase, stuck in a groove of independence versus a rather restricted devolved assembly versus the status quo. Those favouring reform spent more time fighting each other than they did opposing the conservative position.

There had been some interest since the early eighties in trying to resolve the demand for a Scottish legislature by establishing a constitutional convention in order to produce a consensus scheme around which those supporting reform could rally. After the 1987 election, the cross-party Campaign for a Scottish Assembly initiated the Scottish Constitutional Convention through their Claim of Right report. Its function was to bring together Scotland's elected representatives in Westminster and local government with churches, trade unions, political parties, women's organizations and minority ethnic groups in order to see how much agreement could be reached. All but a few local authorities participated, and 63 of the 78 MPs and MEPs. So did Scotland's churches, trade unions and many other organizations. Predictably, the Conservatives would not take part. After initial support for the Convention proposal, the Scottish National Party withdrew before the first meeting. Several different reasons were given, but the most important was probably the fear of compromise blurring their image.

There are a number of distinctive factors about the convention initiative. It has been a genuine attempt to move the constitutional debate away from the uncooperative sectionalism in which it had been confined for the previous twenty years. It brought groups representing important interests into active dialogue with the political parties. It opened up a debate not just about the relationship between Scotland and England but also about the nature of Scottish democracy, and this has distinguished the convention's work from most of the constitutional debate in the previous two decades. Electoral reform, the participation of women, a bill of rights, a democratic parliament, public access – these issues were all addressed in the convention proposals.

Electoral reform was obviously the most difficult. The Labour Party gains substantially from the current electoral system in Scotland, and everyone else loses. Change, therefore, requires one party to sacrifice for the benefit of others. Without the desire to make the convention work, it is unlikely that there would have been any possibility of reform. The trade unions played a crucial role in this process, as did the fact that the churches and other groups as well as the Liberal Democrats favoured change. It was agreed that the additional member system should be used to elect the Scottish parliament. Under this system, 72 members of parliament would be elected under first-past-the-post from the constituencies, and extra seats would be allocated to parties in accordance with the proportion of votes cast for each in each region. As yet there has not been an agreement on the number of additional members.

The problem of women's under-representation in political life was accepted as a central issue, and this stimulated women's groups in Scotland to produce proposals for inclusion in a new constitutional settlement. The most radical of these was for a statutory requirement for gender balance among MPs in a Scottish parliament. There are different methods of achieving this, but what has been agreed is that there will be a statutory requirement on parties to put forward an equal number of male and female candidates. This is simple to achieve among the additional members but more complex among the constituency members. It may be done by pairing constituencies and/or obliging parties to present a male and female candidate in each. The most likely sanction to be applied if parties fail to do this is that they are disqualified from receiving any share of the additional members' seats. Other proposals for hours of work, care facilities, gender balance in public appointments have been readily accepted. The challenge this will present to the parties will be to attract and develop new women entrants into formal political institutions. Scotland, like other places, has many able and experienced women, but they are to be found more frequently in the voluntary organizations than in government agencies or as MPs.

It has been agreed that the parliament will have the power to implement its own bill of rights. Indeed, a prototype already exists in the shape of a draft bill produced by the Scottish Council for Civil Liberties.

Political scientists have long been concerned with the internal structures of legislatures and their relationship with the executive. This could not be described as a common concern among the electorate as a whole, but there are good reasons why it should be. The excessive concentration of power in the executive makes the Westminster political process less responsive to democratic pressures and precludes a more positive contribution from back-bench MPs. Public access to the political process is largely confined to casework on personal problems and party choice at elections. Only the very well organized with professional lobbyists can have some hope of contributing to the policy process. The under-representation of important sections of society in addition to women has been a neglected problem in contemporary democracies.

These were issues which influenced the convention decisions on the internal structures of a Scottish parliament. There was support for a strong committee system with not only powers of investigation and policy review but also some power to initiate legislation. Committees would be expected to go out to different areas of the country to take evidence, particularly seeking those groups less represented within formal structures. The legislature would have substantially more power over its timetable and procedures than Westminster. The hope, which can never be legislated for, is that the combination of a more representative electoral system and a strong committee system will encourage less rigid party relationships than at present. There has also been agreement on a right of petition whereby parliament would be required to debate an issue following a request made by a specified number of signatories.

What does this recent Scottish experience illustrate and what are the implications for the rest of the United Kingdom? Certainly we can see in Scotland that constitutional change can enter the political mainstream and be accepted. The preconditions for this were both the popular perception that the system was failing to satisfy people's democratic aspirations, with real consequences for their lives, and the existence of committed organizations giving coherent form to popular discontent. There has been disagreement about the causal direction of this relationship. Those hostile to reform in Scotland and elsewhere resort to the familiar argument that it is the 'chattering classes', the organized groups with a vested interest in discontent, who manufacture the desire for change. However, the reformers are a product of their own culture and there has been no dichotomy between the people and activists in terms of the direction of change. Opinion polls do show quite consistently that people place such issues as health, employment, housing, considerably above a Scottish parliament when asked to prioritize these issues. But constitutional issues are by their nature instrumental; they are a means of achieving other objectives.

Although we have only partially succeeded in creating a consensus among pro-reform groups (the withdrawal of the SNP left a major division), there has been agreement among quite a wide range of groups, and many people now feel more comfortable about coalition politics. The experience of the convention has been that consensus does not mean the lowest common denominator. Finding agreement has more often required innovation. The participation of non-party groups has been positive and indicates that the concept of social partnership is one which should be developed beyond the formula of government, business and unions, and should actively involve other institutions and the voluntary sector.

The implications for the rest of the United Kingdom are potentially very great. Although Wales has received no commitment from the Labour Party to introduce early legislation for a Welsh assembly, it is unlikely that the setting up of a Scottish parliament would not act as a stimulus in Wales. Even more interesting might be the effect on Northern Ireland. There are sections of both communities who would welcome the establishment of an assembly if the right formula could be agreed. If Scotland had a legislature, Northern Ireland might find it easier to emulate that example rather than feel that it was acting in isolation. The real problem is England. Would it find it acceptable to have an English parliament within a federal structure, or is there some genuine potential for English regionalism? Constitutional change in Scotland may be the key element which brings that debate to life.

We should not be afraid of allowing change to take place in an apparently untidy way. Short of great traumas like war, long-established states are not likely to reinvent themselves from scratch. This is not to deny the value of constitutional models as a guide which may inform the direction of change. But once major change takes place in one part of the system, it invites or requires change in other parts. This change may be asymmetrical, and traditional pragmatism should be able to accommodate that. We should see this as an evolving process – a decade of change in which reformers in different parts of the United Kingdom build on the work of each other. If Scotland makes a breakthrough, will others be far behind?

25 Education for Citizenship

Gus John

The question of how we equip our children to be effective citizens and active participants in civil society has recently become an issue for those planning the school curriculum. The Education Reform Act of 1988 established a national curriculum for all schools in England and Wales. Education for citizenship was subsequently adopted by the National Curriculum Council (NCC) as one of five cross-curricular themes. This means it is not a subject in its own right but should be worked into other subject areas – whether English, maths or science – wherever possible. As defined by the chairman of the National Curriculum Council, Duncan Graham, education for citizenship helps each pupil to 'understand the duties, responsibilities and rights of every citizen and promotes concern for the values by which a civilised society is identified – justice, democracy, respect for the rule of law'.[1] This might seem an entirely laudable goal, but the approach to education for citizenship currently on offer raises a number of important questions.

The first one is at what age or at what particular point in a person's development they can be deemed to have completed their citizenship education. It is assumed that education for citizenship is largely a matter for schoolchildren, yet many adults have little knowledge of their rights and responsibilities and lack basic citizenship skills. While a majority of resources goes into the school system, whether at primary or secondary level, education is essentially a process that goes on throughout life. It should therefore be possible for every individual to continue to engage with education, especially state education, throughout his or her life. By engagement I mean not simply involvement in the sense of consumers of a curriculum, but as people who use their experiences and share them with others.

The tendency over the last ten years in education has been to encourage young people to adopt values and attitudes to do with work, training and the progress of the economy. The microchip revolution effectively means that many more people are leaving the formal working system earlier. The training and education needs and aspirations of these people are seen as somewhat peripheral to the major concerns of the education agenda. For example, it is up to local education authorities to determine whether or not to continue with non-vocational adult educational programmes, but government financial controls make continuation virtually impossible. Local authorities' main statutory obligation is to provide education for 5–18-year-olds. When resources are restricted, adult education is the first casualty. For many, then, education remains a lost opportunity. A credible policy for education for citizenship should, I believe, be concerned with these problems and, indeed, the many other ways in which people's life chances are constrained.

Second, the prevailing ethos is that education should be geared towards individual achievement, rather than recognize education for liberation and education for social justice as important goals. If that is the case, how can the system hope to encourage those 'values by which a civilised society is identified'? Or are we happy to take the cult of the individual as the hallmark of a civilized democracy?

This is linked to the growing tendency towards a market approach to education, which has major implications for education rights and entitlements. Although cloaked in the language of greater choice and rising standards, this approach shows every sign of further undermining educational entitlements rather than delivering them for the majority of disadvantaged groups in society. A market in education creates winners and losers, with resources following a minority of pupils to the most successful schools, leaving most children with an even more demoralized and underfunded service. According to the NCC, education for citizenship aims to 'establish the importance of positive, participative citizenship and provide motivation to join in'.[2] What hope is there of this, if many children are treated as second-class citizens within the education system itself?

This leads us on to the key question of who defines what values we should encourage in citizenship education and with what objective in mind. The NCC's guidelines portray the process as a neutral, uncontentious exercise. Yet far from being timeless, universal principles, the kinds of value promoted in schools clearly depend to a large extent on the social structures within which we all operate and the dominant ideology of the day. Having lived in Britain for 27 years, my experience is that since the 1960s citizenship has increasingly become bound up with issues of nationality and Britishness: who belongs and who does not. For example, the 1981 British Nationality Act created three categories of citizenship: British, British dependent territories and British overseas. It abolished the automatic right to British citizenship for those born on British soil (unless at least one parent was a British citizen or was settled in the United Kingdom at the time of the child's birth) and for Commonwealth citizens settled here before 1973. The 1988 Immigration Act removed the statutory right to family unity: the right of British men and long-settled Commonwealth citizen men to bring their wives and families to the United Kingdom. This followed a ruling in the European Court of Human Rights that UK immigration law discriminated against women, who were not allowed the right to be joined by their husbands. Rather than extend the right of family unity to women, the government removed it altogether. Countless other pieces of legislation have imposed ever more racist immigration controls. The government, then, has it within its power to decide who are to be citizens and what class of citizenship they enjoy. In addition, it has the power to deny citizenship to increasing numbers of people who previously had a legitimate claim to it.

It is a pity that education does not begin by asking itself what it really means to be British in these islands today. How does a young black person or a Kurdish refugee begin to get a sense of belonging when society defines him or her as deficient, problem-causing, somehow marginal to mainstream life and values? But even raising such issues in the classroom could land one in trouble. The 1986 Education Act prohibited the promotion of 'partisan political views' among pupils. We are expected to educate for citizenship while steering away from issues which are considered political or ideological and thus outside the mainstream curriculum. Instead, we must pursue education as if it is some sort of politically neutral activity. Education finds ways of managing the crises – managing behaviour and discipline in the classroom, addressing issues of the participation of parents of black pupils or the aspirations of working-class white pupils as if these issues are completely divorced from unequal social relations. The history syllabus of the national curriculum seeks to displace a hundred and fifty years at least of that part of British social history which has been about struggles for social justice and human liberation. Ending in 1960, the syllabus thus obscures the recent history of the black communities in Britain. The result is that education does not even begin to address the fundamental questions of young people's lives: the struggles they are involved in within their communities, the impact of poverty and unemployment in their family life, and so on.

It is quite facile to organize education and schooling as if the experiences young people have in their day-to-day lives have nothing to do with education as such. For the majority of underachieving black pupils in inner-city areas, day-to-day experiences are about having their fundamental rights and civic entitlements trampled upon. Nowhere in the national curriculum are these experiences addressed. And we would seek to instruct these youngsters in respecting the rights of others, about duties and responsibilities.

If the aim is really to encourage a culture of participative citizenship, then we need to show that the structures for this are in place throughout society. As it is, our children will grow up to be subjects rather than citizens, their rights conditional on the benevolence of whichever political party is in power at the time. A new constitutional settlement with a bill of rights and a written constitution must enshrine the right to a free, high-quality education. The constitutional right of entry to education at any point in one's life should also be enshrined. Furthermore, we need a definition of citizenship which is inclusive rather than exclusive, which recognizes the barriers to participation and seeks to pull them down.

Far from increasing efforts to prevent the infringement of young black people's rights, we witness the increasing transfer of power to those who would deny them. People like myself, who campaigned for yeas against the practice of police going into schools and being given information freely about pupils and their parents, now hear the government saying that the police should be given access by all means. Many police officers now feel it is their right to gain access to schools and take part in the formal delivery of the curriculum and in the informal life of the school. The experiences young people have had of being criminalized, on the streets, in their neighbourhoods, in their homes and elsewhere, for anything from riding bicycles without lights to being suspected of intent to commit offences is not taken into consideration. But while schools prefer to ignore the issue, it has a huge impact on the attitudes of the young. Young people soon dismiss many of the values we seek to inculcate in them as hypocritical and oppressive, and subscribe to a different code.

In 1981, I was the chair of the Moss Side Defence Committee in Manchester, following the mass uprisings of mainly young people, black and white, in the streets in the Rusholme and Moss Side districts. The response of the authorities was harsh. The police and the courts were attempting to prove that they had it in their power to retaliate and that the system had not broken down. Sitting in the courts with many of those young people, they would say to me: 'We've organised our defence to win, but if we don't you shouldn't feel too sad. As far as we're concerned we have nothing to lose. We are not going to subscribe to the values of the teachers and the rest of them.'

Until such time as education for citizenship encompasses these issues within its agenda, takes account of the type of society we are creating and the way certain groups of young people are being systematically dispossessed within it, it will do little more than provide a basic introduction to 'civics', anachronistic as that obviously is. If we want a meaningful process of education for citizenship, we should forget about the national curriculum and the Education Reform Act. Recent education policy has dismissed completely twenty-five years of struggle around the issue of black education rights, and around the need to enhance white working-class educational aspirations and outcomes. We need to draw on past struggles and devise much more radical approaches to addressing the fundamental issues of Britishness, class, race and gender, and of the power relationships they engender within society. Education for citizenship has to be about the legitimation of those issues and struggles in curriculum planning and delivery. This in turn depends on whether we lay the foundations now for a genuine culture of citizenship, in which rights and entitlements are extended to the least powerful in our society.

Notes

1 D. Graham, *Curriculum Guidance 8: Education for Citizenship* (National Curriculum Council, York, 1990), foreword.
2 Ibid., p. 2.

26 Imagining a Democratic Culture

Marina Warner

'The political institutions of any nation are always menaced and are ultimately controlled by the spiritual state of that nation' – so wrote James Baldwin, in *The Fire Next Time*. By spiritual, he did not mean anything religious, but the life of the spirit: we have a right to that life, to the vitality of imagination, of expression, to the fulfilment of gifts, to skills and to pleasure. Constitutions can also enshrine this basic human right. The revolutionary Enlightenment formula of Thomas Jefferson – 'the pursuit of happiness' – could be interpreted in this way. And Baldwin is right when he declares that this cannot be split off from the institutions and sites of power and authority: this is why the demands that our charter makes include a vision of how things might be, in the broadest possible human terms, including matters of culture.

One of the many, many damaging developments of the last decade or so has been the drip-fed notion that art is something fandangled, weird, vaguely unsavoury and antisocial, or otherwise off limits: a luxury for intellectuals, or for business cartels in block-booked seats at Glyndebourne. The impoverishment we have seen is not simply material – though this has been desperate, especially among women and children. It has been immaterial as well, cultural and spiritual.

Culture is the social face of the polis, and it has assimilated the old function of religion to some extent, of religio, or re-binding together, recombining. I do not believe that literature or art or music make people good: I know that writers and artists can be brutes and worse. I am well aware that books and writings can be used to incite as well as to illuminate: Mussolini began as a journalist, which is why the first thing he did, like all those who seek undemocratic power, was to shut down the press. But I am completely committed to the belief that culture is the voice and the face of the people, and as such it needs, just like civil rights and legal justice, to be cared for and upheld, and listened to, not left to its own devices. For in a world of mass communication and multinational-corporations, it cannot be in command of its own devices without help.

As arts, as entertainment, as pleasure and diversion, as a tonic to the spirit and light in the imagination, culture should be available in practice to every citizen; not just a right on paper. This brings me to a crucial aspect of culture if it is to be democratic: access to it and representation within it. Participation is the key to this: so that the culture embraces all the diversity and well-being of its readers, spectators, audiences, as well as the situation of the artists themselves in different media. The so-called free market-place is not the way to achieve this constellation of different audiences and needs. Like majority rule in Parliament, it creates a spurious majority taste, usually based in the metropolis, and then goes on reinforcing it. A 'national culture' is a monolithic and ultimately Stalinist notion; besides, it is unworkable in the diverse society of Britain.

A multi-vocal, democratic culture is, however, not made up of national ethnic islets of separate indentities that hark back to distinct histories, determined by appeal to former geographies, languages, religion and customs. Frequently the appeal to tradition denies the culture of others, and in its claim to uniqueness refuses the freedom that allows us to be and become different.

The complexities and variety of British society are one of our richest resources, but we risk wasting this wealth if we do not let our culture thrive from within, so that language flowers in the mouths of citizens, rather than be poured down their throats. Culture is like friendship in that respect: it tends to grow in the making, exponentially, through further contacts, shared endeavour, deepening conversation, longer trust. A friendship, like culture, depends on understanding particularity and difference, on developing empathy and understanding. Selling an American series to a national network for children's hour can never match a programme made locally, which pays attention to the character of the audience. Yet in the area of film, possibly the most popular and powerful medium of cultural expression ever known, with a shelf life now prolonged by video and satellite beyond all expectation, the Europeans, Britain included, have virtually abandoned the struggle with Hollywood. Some of our preoccupations and problems resemble America's, but through film we could imagine other ways of dealing with them. We could tell ourselves another story, a story that meets the needs of our circle of listeners and spectators. We could tell it in a babel of tongues – many of them English, but an English that in its very utterance creates a new history, a new perspective. Angela Carter's last novel, *Wise Children*, takes Shakespeare back to his sources in popular folklore and storytelling, in popular entertainment, and incidentally creates on the way a comic novel of ethnic manners – in this case, the manners of South London, *c.*1900 to the present day: the Brit bred in the bone is observed as a species from the inside, a truly modern experiment, reversing the orientalist position of holding up 'foreigners' for wonderstruck scrutiny.

The question is not how to guard a national identity, but how to live plurality organically: to live with a breathing, growing, changing organism. The boundaries of this organism are no longer geographical – the islands of the Uinted Kingdom – or in our case linguistic – English has become the Latin of the modern world, the unifying common language of literature and thought. Many writers, from India, Africa, the West Indies, choose to write in English, as a universal language, marvellously rich and supple and changeable, offering them not the ditch of colonialism in which to lay themselves down, but a seedbed to grow with their own rich crops. An anthology like *The Penguin Book of Caribbean Verse* reveals how inappropriate it is to think of the English language as a possession of Britain: the post-colonial country no longer has mastery, and its historical connection to its mother tongue does not grant it exclusive authority over it. To quote James Baldwin again: 'To accept one's past – one's history, is not the same thing as drowning in it; it is learning how to use it.'

We need to learn to use our history, and make a new myth to live by. Only by examining the old myths can we start its creation. Charter 88 is a beginning, because it grows out of traditions but seeks to change them profoundly. It may succeed because of our new international situation. History has positioned Britain facing two ways: towards America, because of language, above all (though political alliance obviously plays a part), and towards Europe. In spite of notorious insularity, cultural affinities with the mainland have always existed and can be built on: from the dissemination of the medieval romances, like the story of Tristan and Isolde, which carries its protagonists to Cornwall, to the deep sympathy of the Romantics with German philosophy, we have shared much more with the continentals than we own up to, and one aspect of strengthened European links would be to uncover our shared history in order to help a new one to flourish.

To illustrate my idea of a culture that acknowledges diversity and combines it into a strength, I would like to be utopian for a moment. Diaspora seems to me to be the modern condition: men and women all over Europe – not just Britain – have arrived from somewhere else, sometimes a long while ago, sometimes recently. These migrations will continue: there will be more refugees, more political fugitives, more men and women simply moving on in the search for work and the comparative freedom work grants.

Separatism, ethnic self-assertion form one response to this diaspora: identity through preserving culture and religion; but it does not seem to me the best response to the difficulties of living the diaspora, any more than Hassidism has helped the peace movement in Israel – or for that matter in New York. We are aware that for every British Muslim who supported the *fatwa* against Salman Rushdie, there were many who did not, who were indeed faithful Friday attenders at the mosque but were embarrassed or revolted by the call to violence – just as I was ashamed by so many measures taken by the Tories in the name of the professional classes to which I belong.

The poet Tom Paulin, in a fine essay,[1] produced a phrase that has tremendous resonance for me, and opens up the idea I want to offer you here. Writing about the poet Elizabeth Bishop, he said she tries to create in her poetry 'Dwellings without roots'. He describes how in her poems, about Latin America especially, she tries to undo the conquistador's authority in her imagery and her language, set aside the baggage of colonial and imperialist complacency, and evolve instead a vocabulary of transience, fragility, impermanence, which pays proper tribute to the disappeared ones who were as much part of history and culture as the names carved in stone on the monuments. Bishop is by no means the only writer engaged in this task: the poet George Lamming wrote in his book *The Pleasures of Exile* that Caliban and Miranda share something in common, after all. They have both had their pasts abolished: they share an ignorance which is also the source of some vision. It is as it were a kind of creative blindness. The loss of their mothers – Sycorax the 'witch' in Caliban's case, a nameless and indeed featureless woman in Miranda's case – can represent the loss of roots, the predicament of exile, of deracination, for which another word is diaspora.

In the process of uttering, or writing, or representing – out of uprootedness, out of unbelonging – artists can create new dwellings with their memory and imagination. But they need not plant them again on the foundations and ruins of the old, but set them up instead like nomads' tents, pitched by a new oasis. Such dwellings have bases which exist in imagination and memory, but they also put out new cells which themselves become the foundations, the floors of a new dwelling: this is an image, perhaps, for the way a democratic culture may grow.

In practical terms, how can it be achieved? I could make a list of the necessary conditions and it would include all the big needs: more social mobility, more education, more school as well as high-street libraries, regulation of and investment in public interest broadcasting, investment in the cinema. To this I would add that existing cultural institutions should become much more accessible. Existing buildings should be used, especially when standing idle, like schools during the holidays.

Above all, the new phenomenon of the age, 'the child consumer', should be paid close attention. A 1991 report, *Children – The Influencing Factor*, reveals that in all social classes, children between 5 and 12 are having the greatest effect on their parents' buying patterns. Witness the green revolution in our supermarkets as more children become ecologists and vegetarians. 'Pester power', the adspeople call it: between now and 2000, this group in the population is going to rise by 13 per cent, compared to 3 per cent of the rest of the population. In an imagined democratic culture of the future, children would not be treated as consumers only, but their energies and imaginations would contribute to the making of the culture. They are the audience and the artists, but they are being neglected. Many of them, born in Britain, from different backgrounds of country, faith and, in some cases, language, are living the diaspora. They could help pitch the tent, craft the new dwellings, praise what is to be praised in the past without sinking in it, and drowning.

So the charter's campaign to make every member of society a citizen not a subject applies to culture too. The curious, deeply hopeful aspect of the matter is that the very difficulties we are living through can be turned creatively into raised voices, thrown across the rooms of our new dwellings.

Notes

1   T. Paulin, *Minotaur: Poetry and the Nation State* (Faber London, 1992).